BTEC National
Media

Study Guide

A PEARSON COMPANY

BTEC National Study Guide: Media

Published by:
Edexcel Limited
One90 High Holborn
London WC1V 7BH
www.edexcel.org.uk

Distributed by:
Pearson Education Limited
Edinburgh Gate
Harlow
Essex CM20 2JE

First published 2007

ISBN 978-1-84690-220-8

Project managed and typeset by Hart McLeod, Cambridge
Printed in Great Britain by Henry Ling Ltd., at the Dorset Press, Dorchester, Dorset

Cover image ©Carsten Reisinger/Alamy

The publisher's policy is to use paper manufactured from sustainable forests.

Acknowledgements
p.43 ©Image Source Pink/Getty Images; p.44 ©Mykel Nicolaou/Rex Features; p.48 ©ITV/Rex Features; p.49 ©Moodboard/Corbis; p.52 ©Tyler Sableford/Photographer's Choice/Getty Images; p.85 ©Gabe Palmer/Corbis; p.87 ©Joe Cornish/Arcaid/Corbis; p.89 ©Paul Thompson/Corbis

Contents

PREFACE

If you've already followed a BTEC First programme, you will know that this is an exciting way to study; if you are fresh from GCSEs you will find that from now on you will be in charge of your own learning. This guide has been written specially for you, to help get you started and then succeed on your BTEC National course.

The **Introduction** concentrates on making sure you have all the right facts about your course at your fingertips. Also, it guides you through the important skills you need to develop if you want to do well including:

- managing your time
- researching information
- preparing a presentation.

Keep this by your side throughout your course and dip into it whenever you need to.

The **Activities** give you tasks to do on your own, in a small group or as a class. They will help you internalise your learning and then prepare for assessment by practising your skills and showing you how much you know. These activities are not for assessment.

The sample **Marked Assignments** show you what other students have done to gain Pass, Merit or Distinction. By seeing what past students have done, you should be able to improve your own grade.

Your BTEC National will cover six, twelve or eighteen units depending on whether you are doing an Award, Certificate or Diploma. In this guide the activities cover sections from Unit 1 – Research Techniques for the Media Industries, Unit 2 – Pre-Production Techniques for the Media Industries, Unit 3 – Production Management Project and Unit 4 – Working to a Brief in the Media Industries. These units underpin your study of Media.

Because the guide covers only four units, it is essential that you do all the other work your tutors set you. You will have to research information in textbooks, in the library and on the Internet. You should have the opportunity to visit local organisations and welcome visiting speakers to your institution. This is a great way to find out more about your chosen vocational area – the type of jobs that are available and what the work is really like.

This Guide is a taster, an introduction to your BTEC National. Use it as such and make the most of the rich learning environment that your tutors will provide for you. Your BTEC National will give you an excellent base for further study, a broad understanding of business and the knowledge you need to succeed in the world of work. Remember, thousands of students have achieved a BTEC National and are now studying for a degree or at work, building a successful career.

INTRODUCTION

SEVEN STEPS TO SUCCESS ON YOUR BTEC NATIONAL

You have received this guide because you have decided to do a BTEC National qualification. You may even have started your course. At this stage you should feel good about your decision. BTEC Nationals have many benefits – they are well-known and respected qualifications, they provide excellent preparation for future work or help you to get into university if that is your aim. If you are already at work then gaining a BTEC National will increase your value to your employer and help to prepare you for promotion.

Despite all these benefits though, you may be rather apprehensive about your ability to cope. Or you may be wildly enthusiastic about the whole course! More probably, you are somewhere between the two – perhaps quietly confident most of the time but sometimes worried that you may get out of your depth as the course progresses. You may be certain you made the right choice or still have days when your decision worries you. You may understand exactly what the course entails and what you have to do – or still feel rather bewildered, given all the new stuff you have to get your head around.

Your tutors will use the induction sessions at the start of your course to explain the important information they want you to know. At the time, though, it can be difficult to remember everything. This is especially true if you have just left school and are now studying in a new environment, among a group of people you have only just met. It is often only later that you think of useful questions to ask. Sometimes, misunderstandings or difficulties may only surface weeks or months into a course – and may continue for some time unless they are quickly resolved.

Make sure you have all the right facts

This student guide has been written to help to minimise these difficulties, so that you get the most out of your BTEC National course from day one. You can read through it at your own pace. You can look back at it whenever you have a problem or query.

This Introduction concentrates on making sure you have all the right facts about your course at your fingertips. This includes a **Glossary** (on page 32) which explains the specialist terms you may hear or read – including words and phrases highlighted in bold type in this Introduction.

The Introduction also guides you through the important skills you need to develop if you want to do well – such as managing your time, researching information and preparing a presentation; as well as reminding you about the key skills you will need to do justice to your work, such as good written and verbal communications.

- Use the PlusPoint boxes in each section to help you to stay focused on the essentials.
- Use the Action Point boxes to check out things you need to know or do right now.
- Refer to the Glossary (on page 32) if you need to check the meaning of any of the specialist terms you may hear or read.

Remember, thousands of students have achieved BTEC National Diplomas and are now studying for a degree or at work, building a successful career. Many were nervous and unsure of themselves at the outset – and very few experienced absolutely no setbacks during the course. What they did have, though, was a belief in their own ability to do well if they concentrated on getting things right one step at a time. This Introduction enables you to do exactly the same!

STEP ONE

UNDERSTAND YOUR COURSE AND HOW IT WORKS

What is a BTEC qualification and what does it involve? What will you be expected to do on the course? What can you do afterwards? How does this National differ from 'A' levels or a BTEC First qualification?

All these are common questions – but not all prospective students ask them! Did you? And, if so, did you really listen to the answers? And can you remember them now?

If you have already completed a BTEC First course then you may know some of the answers – although you may not appreciate some of the differences between that course and your new one.

Let's start by checking out the basics.

- All BTEC National qualifications are **vocational** or **work-related**. This doesn't mean that they give you all the skills that you need to do a job. It does mean that you gain the specific knowledge and understanding relevant to your chosen subject or area of work. This means that when you start in a job you will learn how to do the work more quickly and should progress further. If you are already employed, it means you become more valuable to your employer. You can choose to study a BTEC National in a wide range of vocational areas, such as Business, Health and Social Care, IT, Performing Arts and many others.
- There are three types of BTEC National qualification and each has a different number of units.
  - The BTEC National Award usually has 6 units and takes 360 **guided learning hours (GLH)** to complete. It is often offered as a part-time or short course but you may be one of the many students doing an Award alongside A-levels as a full-time course. An Award is equivalent to one 'A' level.
  - The BTEC National Certificate usually has 12 units and takes 720 GLH to complete. You may be able to study for the Certificate on a part-time or full-time course. It is equivalent to two 'A' levels.

- The BTEC National Diploma usually has 18 units and takes 1080 GLH to complete. It is normally offered as a two-year full-time course. It is equivalent to three 'A' levels.

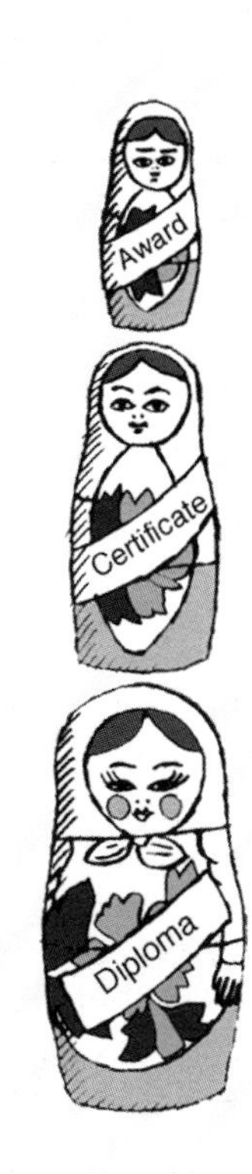

These qualifications are often described as **nested**. This means that they fit inside each other (rather like Russian dolls!) because the same units are common to them all. This means that if you want to progress from one to another you can do so easily by simply completing more units.

- Every BTEC National qualification has a set number of **core units**. These are the compulsory units every student must complete. The number of core units you will do on your course depends upon the vocational area you are studying.
- All BTEC National qualifications also have a range of **specialist units** from which you may be able to make a choice. These enable you to study particular areas in more depth.
- Some BTEC National qualifications have **specialist core units**. These are mandatory units you will have to complete if you want to follow a particular pathway in certain vocational areas. Engineering is an example of a qualification with the overarching title, Engineering, which has a set of core units that all students must complete. Then, depending what type of engineering a student wants to follow, there are more specialist core units that must be studied.
- On all BTEC courses you are expected to be in charge of your own learning. If you have completed a BTEC First, you will already have been introduced to this idea, but you can expect the situation to be rather different now that you are working at BTEC National level. Students on a BTEC First course will be expected to need more guidance whilst they develop their skills and find their feet. In some cases, this might last quite some time. On a BTEC National course you will be expected to take more responsibility for yourself and your own learning almost from the outset. You will quickly be expected to start thinking for yourself. This means planning what to do and carrying out a task without needing constant reminders. This doesn't mean that your tutor won't give you help and guidance when you need it. It does mean, though, that you need to be 'self-starting' and to be able to use your own initiative. You also need to be able to assess your own performance and make improvements when necessary. If you enjoy having the freedom to make your own decisions and work at your own pace then you will welcome this type of learning with open arms. However, there are dangers! If you are a procrastinator (look up this word if you don't know what it means!) then it's quite likely you will quickly get in a muddle. In this case read Step 3 – Use your time wisely – very carefully indeed!
- The way you are assessed and graded on a BTEC course is different from an 'A' level course, although you will still obtain UCAS points which you need if you want to go to university. You can read about this in the next section.

PLUSPOINTS

+ You can usually choose to study part-time or full-time for your BTEC National and do an Award, Certificate or Diploma and progress easily from one to the other.
+ You will study both core units and specialist units on your course.
+ When you have completed your BTEC course you can get a job (or **apprenticeship**), use your qualification to develop your career and/or continue your studies to degree level.
+ You are responsible for your own learning on a BTEC course. This prepares you for life at work or at university when you will be expected to be self-starting and to use your own initiative.

ACTION POINTS

✓ Check you know whether you are studying for an Award, Certificate or Diploma and find out the number of units you will be studying for your BTEC National qualification.

✓ Find out which are core and which are specialist units, and which specialist units are offered at your school or college.

✓ Check out the length of your course and when you will be studying each unit.

✓ Explore the Edexcel website at www.edexcel.org.uk. Your first task is to find what's available for your particular BTEC National qualification. Start by finding National qualifications, then look for your vocational area and check you are looking at the 2007 schemes. Then find the specification for your course. Don't print this out – it is far too long. You could, of course, save it if you want to refer to it regularly or you could just look through it for interest and then bookmark the pages relating to your qualification for future reference.

✓ Score yourself out of 5 (where 0 is awful and 5 is excellent) on each of the following to see how much improvement is needed for you to become responsible for your own learning!

Being punctual; organisational ability; tidiness; working accurately; finding and correcting own mistakes; solving problems; accepting responsibility; working with details; planning how to do a job; using own initiative; thinking up new ideas; meeting deadlines.

✓ Draw up your own action plan to improve any areas where you are weak. Talk this through at your next individual **tutorial**.

STEP TWO

UNDERSTAND HOW YOU ARE ASSESSED AND GRADED – AND USE THIS KNOWLEDGE TO YOUR ADVANTAGE!

If you already have a BTEC First qualification, you may think that you don't need to read this section because you assume that BTEC National is simply more of the same. Whilst there are some broad similarities, you will now be working at an entirely different level and the grades you get for your work could be absolutely crucial to your future plans.

Equally, if you have opted for BTEC National rather than 'A' level because you thought you would have less work (or writing) to do then you need to read this section very carefully. Indeed, if you chose your BTEC National because you thought it would guarantee you an easy life, you are likely to get quite a shock when reality hits home!

It is true that, unlike 'A' levels, there are no exams on a BTEC course. However, to do well you need to understand the importance of your assignments, how these are graded and how these convert into unit points and UCAS points. This is the focus of this section.

Your assignments

On a BTEC National course your learning is assessed by means of **assignments** set by your tutors and given to you to complete throughout your course.

- Your tutors will use a variety of **assessment methods**, such as case studies, projects, presentations and shows to obtain evidence of your skills and knowledge to date. You may also be given work-based or **time-constrained** assignments – where your performance might be observed and assessed. It will depend very much on the vocational area you are studying (see also page 16).

- Important skills you will need to learn are how to research information (see page 25) and how to use your time effectively, particularly if you have to cope with several assignments at the same time (see page 12). You may also be expected to work cooperatively as a member of a team to complete some parts of your assignments – especially if you are doing a subject like Performing Arts – or to prepare a presentation (see page 26).
- All your assignments are based on **learning outcomes** set by Edexcel. These are listed for each unit in your course specification. You have to meet *all* the learning outcomes to pass the unit.

Your grades

On a BTEC National course, assignments that meet the learning outcomes are graded as Pass, Merit or Distinction.

- The difference between these grades has very little to do with how much you write! Edexcel sets out the **grading criteria** for the different grades in a **grading grid**. This identifies the **higher-level skills** you have to demonstrate to earn a higher grade. You can find out more about this, and read examples of good (and not so good) answers to assignments at Pass, Merit and Distinction level in the assessed assignments section starting on page 95. You will also find out more about getting the best grade you can in Step 5 – Understand your assessment – on page 16.
- Your grades for all your assignments earn you **unit points**. The number of points you get for each unit is added together and your total score determines your final grade(s) for the qualification – again either Pass, Merit or Distinction. You get one final grade if you are taking a BTEC National Award, two if you are taking a BTEC National Certificate and three if you are taking a BTEC National Diploma.
- Your points and overall grade(s) also convert to **UCAS points** which you will need if you want to apply to study on a degree course. As an example, if you are studying a BTEC National Diploma, and achieve three final pass grades you will achieve 120 UCAS points. If you achieve three final distinction grades the number of UCAS points you have earned goes up to 360.
- It is important to note that you start earning both unit and UCAS points from the very first assignment you complete! This means that if you take a long time to settle into your course, or to start working productively, you could easily lose valuable points for quite some time. If you have your heart set on a particular university or degree course then this could limit your choices. Whichever way you look at it, it is silly to squander potentially good grades for an assignment and their equivalent points, just because you didn't really understand what you had to do – which is why this guide has been written to help you!
- If you take a little time to understand how **grade boundaries** work,

you can see where you need to concentrate your efforts to get the best final grade possible. Let's give a simple example. Chris and Shaheeda both want to go to university and have worked hard on their BTEC National Diploma course. Chris ends with a total score of 226 unit points which converts to 280 UCAS points. Shaheeda ends with a total score of 228 unit points – just two points more – which converts to 320 UCAS points! This is because a score of between 204 and 227 unit points gives 280 UCAS points, whereas a score of 228 – 251 points gives 320 UCAS points. Shaheeda is pleased because this increases her chances of getting a place on the degree course she wants. Chris is annoyed. He says if he had known then he would have put more effort into his last assignment to get two points more.

- It is always tempting to spend time on work you like doing, rather than work you don't – but this can be a mistake if you have already done the best you can at an assignment and it would already earn a very good grade. Instead you should now concentrate on improving an assignment which covers an area where you know you are weak, because this will boost your overall grade(s). You will learn more about this in Step 3 – Use your time wisely.

PLUSPOINTS

+ Your learning is assessed in a variety of ways, such as by assignments, projects and case studies. You will need to be able to research effectively, manage your own time and work well with other people to succeed.
+ You need to demonstrate specific knowledge and skills to achieve the learning outcomes set by Edexcel. You need to demonstrate you can meet all the learning outcomes to pass a unit.
+ Higher-level skills are required for higher grades. The grading criteria for Pass, Merit and Distinction grades are set out in a grading grid for the unit.
+ The assessment grades of Pass, Merit and Distinction convert to unit points. The total number of unit points you receive during the course determines your final overall grade(s) and the UCAS points you have earned.
+ Working effectively from the beginning maximises your chances of achieving a good qualification grade. Understanding grade boundaries enables you to get the best final grade(s) possible.

ACTION POINTS

✓ Find the learning outcomes for the units you are currently studying. Your tutor may have given you these already, or you can find them in the specification for your course that you already accessed at www.edexcel.org.uk.

✓ Look at the grading grid for the units and identify the way the evidence required changes to achieve the higher grades. Don't worry if there are some words that you do not understand – these are explained in more detail on page 32 of this guide.

✓ If you are still unsure how the unit points system works, ask your tutor to explain it to you.

✓ Check out the number of UCAS points you would need for any course or university in which you are interested.

✓ Keep a record of the unit points you earn throughout your course and check regularly how this is affecting your overall grade(s), based on the grade boundaries for your qualification. Your tutor will give you this information or you can check it yourself in the specification for your course on the Edexcel website.

STEP THREE

USE YOUR TIME WISELY

Most students on a BTEC National course are trying to combine their course commitments with a number of others – such as a job (either full or part-time) and family responsibilities. In addition, they still want time to meet with friends, enjoy a social life and keep up hobbies and interests that they have.

Starting the course doesn't mean that you have to hide away for months if you want to do well. It does mean that you have to use your time wisely if you want to do well, stay sane and keep a balance in your life.

You will only do this if you make time work for you, rather than against you, by taking control. This means that you decide what you are doing, when you are doing it and work purposefully; rather than simply reacting to problems or panicking madly because you've yet another deadline staring you in the face.

Use your time wisely

This becomes even more important as your course progresses because your workload is likely to increase, particularly towards the end of a term. In the early days you may be beautifully organised and able to cope easily. Then you may find you have several tasks to complete simultaneously as well as some research to start. Then you get two assignments in the same week from different tutors – as well as having a presentation to prepare. Then another assignment is scheduled for the following week – and so on. This is not because your tutors are being deliberately difficult. Indeed, most will try to schedule your assignments to avoid such clashes. The problem, of course, is that none of your tutors can assess your abilities until you have learned something – so if several units start and end at the same time it is highly likely there will be some overlap between your assignments.

To cope when the going gets tough, without collapsing into an exhausted heap, you need to learn a few time management skills.

- **Pinpoint where your time goes at the moment** Time is like money – it's usually difficult to work out where it all went! Work out how much time you currently spend at college, at work, at home and on social activities. Check, too, how much time you waste each week – and why this happens. Are you disorganised or do you easily get distracted? Then identify commitments that are vital and those that are optional so that you know where you can find time if you need to.
- **Plan when and where to work** It is unrealistic not to expect to do quite a lot of work for your course in your own time. It is also better to work regularly, and in relatively short bursts, than to work just once or twice a week for very long stretches. In addition to deciding when to work, and for how long, you also need to think about when and where to work. If you are a lark, you will work better early in the day; if you are an owl, you will be at your best later on. Whatever time you work, you need somewhere quiet so that you can concentrate and with space for books and other resources you need. If the words 'quiet oasis' and 'your house' are totally incompatible at any time of the day or night

then check out the opening hours of your local and college library so that you have an escape route if you need it. If you are trying to combine studying with parental responsibilities it is sensible to factor in your children's commitments – and work around their bedtimes too! Store up favours, too, from friends and grandparents that you can call in if you get desperate for extra time when an assignment deadline is looming.

- **Schedule your commitments** Keep a diary or (even better) a wall chart and write down every appointment you make or task you are given. It is useful to use a colour code to differentiate between personal and work or course commitments. You may also want to enter assignment review dates with your tutor in one colour and final deadline dates in another. Keep your diary or chart up-to-date by adding any new dates promptly every time you receive another task or assignment or whenever you make any other arrangements. Keep checking ahead so that you always have prior warning when important dates are looming. This stops you from planning a heavy social week when you will be at your busiest at work or college and from arranging a dental appointment on the morning when you and your team are scheduled to give an important presentation!
- **Prioritise your work** This means doing the most important and urgent task first, rather than the one you like the most! Normally this will be the task or assignment with the nearest deadline. There are two exceptions. Sometimes you may need to send off for information and allow time for it to arrive. It is therefore sensible to do this first so that you are not held up later. The second is when you have to take account of other people's schedules – because you are working in a team or are arranging to interview someone, for example. In this case you will have to arrange your schedule around their needs, not just your own.
- **Set sensible timescales** Trying to do work at the last minute or in a rush is never satisfactory, so it is wise always to allocate more time than you think you will need, never less. Remember, too, to include all the stages of a complex task or assignment, such as researching the information, deciding what to use, creating a first draft, checking it and making improvements and printing it out. If you are planning to do any of your work in a central facility always allow extra time and try to start work early. If you arrive at the last minute you may find every computer and printer is fully utilised until closing time.
- **Learn self-discipline!** This means not putting things off (procrastinating!) because you don't know where to start or don't feel in the mood. Unless you are ill, you have to find some way of persuading yourself to work. One way is to bribe yourself. Make a start and promise yourself that if you work productively for 30 minutes then you deserve a small reward. After 30 minutes you may have become more engrossed and want to keep going a little longer. Otherwise at least you have made a start, so it's easier to come back and do more later. It doesn't matter whether you have research to do, an assignment to write up, a coaching session to plan, or lines to learn, you need to be self-disciplined.
- **Take regular breaks and keep your life in balance** Don't go to the opposite extreme and work for hours on end. Take regular breaks to

give yourself a rest and a change of activity. You need to recharge your batteries! Similarly, don't cancel every social arrangement so that you can work 24/7. Whilst this may be occasionally necessary if you have several deadlines looming simultaneously, it should only be a last resort. If you find yourself doing this regularly then go back to the beginning of this section and see where your time–management planning is going wrong.

PLUSPOINTS

+ Being in control of your time enables you to balance your commitments according to their importance and allows you not let to anyone down – including yourself.
+ Controlling time involves knowing how you spend (and waste!) your time now, planning when best to do work, scheduling your commitments and setting sensible timescales for work to be done.
+ Knowing how to prioritise means that you will schedule work effectively according to its urgency and importance but this also requires self-discipline. You have to follow the schedule you have set for yourself!
+ Managing time and focusing on the task at hand means you will do better work and be less stressed, because you are not having to react to problems or crises. You can also find the time to include regular breaks and leisure activities in your schedule.

ACTION POINTS

✓ Find out how many assignments you can expect to receive this term and when you can expect to receive these. Enter this information into your student diary or onto a planner you can refer to regularly.

✓ Update your diary and/or planner with other commitments that you have this term – both work/college-related and social. Identify any potential clashes and decide the best action to take to solve the problem.

✓ Identify your own best time and place to work quietly and effectively.

✓ Displacement activities are things we do to put off starting a job we don't want to do – such as sending texts, watching TV, checking emails etc. Identify yours so that you know when you're doing them!

STEP FOUR

UTILISE ALL YOUR RESOURCES

Your resources are all the things that can help you to achieve your qualification. They can therefore be as wide-ranging as your favourite website and your **study buddy** (see below) who collects handouts for you if you miss a class.

Your college will provide the essential resources for your course, such as a library with a wide range of books and electronic reference sources, learning resource centre(s), the computer network and Internet access. Other basic resources you will be expected to provide yourself, such as file folders and paper. The policy on textbooks varies from one college to another, but on most courses today students are expected to buy their own. If you look after yours carefully, then you have the option to sell it on to someone else afterwards and recoup some of your money. If you scribble all over it, leave it on the floor and then tread on it, turn back pages and rapidly turn it into a dog-eared, misshapen version of its former self then you miss out on this opportunity.

Unfortunately students often squander other opportunities to utilise resources in the best way – usually because they don't think about them very much, if at all. To help, below is a list of the resources you should consider important – with a few tips on how to get the best out of them.

- **Course information** This includes your course specification, this Study Guide and all the other information relating to your BTEC National which you can find on the Edexcel website. Add to this all the information given to you at college relating to your course, including term dates, assignment dates and, of course, your timetable. This should not be 'dead' information that you glance at once and then discard or ignore. Rather it is important reference material that you need to store somewhere obvious, so that you can look at it whenever you have a query or need to clarify something quickly.
- **Course materials** In this group is your textbook (if there is one), the handouts you are given as well as print-outs and notes you make yourself. File handouts the moment you are given them and put them into an A4 folder bought for the purpose. You will need one for each unit you study. Some students prefer lever-arch files but these are more bulky so more difficult to carry around all day. Unless you have a locker at college it can be easier to keep a lever arch file at home for permanent storage of past handouts and notes for a unit and carry an A4 folder with you which contains current topic information. Filing handouts and print-outs promptly means they don't get lost. They are also less likely to get crumpled, torn or tatty becoming virtually unreadable. Unless you have a private and extensive source of income then this is even more important if you have to pay for every print-out you take in your college resource centre. If you are following a course such as Art and Design, then there will be all your art materials and the pieces you produce. You must look after these with great care.
- **Other stationery items** Having your own pens, pencils, notepad, punch, stapler and sets of dividers is essential. Nothing irritates tutors more than watching one punch circulate around a group – except, perhaps, the student who trudges into class with nothing to write on or with. Your dividers should be clearly labelled to help you store and find notes, print-outs and handouts fast. Similarly, your notes should be clearly headed and dated. If you are writing notes up from your own research then you will have to include your source. Researching information is explained in Step 6 – Sharpen your skills.
- **Equipment and facilities** These include your college library and resource centres, the college computer network and other college equipment you can use, such as laptop computers, photocopiers and presentation equipment. Much of this may be freely available; others – such as using the photocopier in the college library or the printers in a resource centre – may cost you money. Many useful resources will be electronic, such as DVDs or electronic journals and databases. At home you may have your own computer with Internet access to count as a resource. Finally, include any specialist equipment and facilities available for your particular course that you use at college or have at home.

Utilise all your resources

All centralised college resources and facilities are invaluable if you know how to use them – but can be baffling when you don't. Your induction should have included how to use the library, resource centre(s) and computer network. You should also have been informed of the policy on using IT equipment which determines what you can and can't do when you are using college computers. If, by any chance, you missed this then go and check it out for yourself. Library and resource centre staff will be only too pleased to give you helpful advice – especially if you pick a quiet time to call in. You can also find out about the allowable ways to transfer data between your college computer and your home computer if your options are limited because of IT security.

Having a study buddy is a good idea

- **People** You are surrounded by people who are valuable resources: your tutor(s), specialist staff at college, your employer and work colleagues, your relatives and any friends who have particular skills or who work in the same area you are studying. Other members of your class are also useful resources – although they may not always seem like it! Use them, for example, to discuss topics out of class time. A good debate between a group of students can often raise and clarify issues that there may not be time to discuss fully in class. Having a study buddy is another good idea – you get/make notes for them when they are away and vice versa. That way you don't miss anything.

  If you want information or help from someone, especially anyone outside your immediate circle, then remember to get the basics right! Approach them courteously, do your homework first so that you are well-prepared and remember that you are asking for assistance – not trying to get them to do the work for you! If someone has agreed to allow you to interview them as part of your research for an assignment or project then good preparations will be vital, as you will see in Step 6 – Sharpen your Skills (see page 22).

  One word of warning: be wary about using information from friends or relatives who have done a similar or earlier course. First, the slant of the material they were given may be different. It may also be out-of-date. And *never* copy anyone else's written assignments. This is **plagiarism** – a deadly sin in the educational world. You can read more about this in Step 5 – Understand your assessment (see page 16).

- **You!** You have the ability to be your own best resource or your own worst enemy! The difference depends upon your work skills, your personal skills and your attitude to your course and other people. You have already seen how to use time wisely. Throughout this guide you will find out how to sharpen and improve other work and personal skills and how to get the most out of your course – but it is up to you to read it and apply your new-found knowledge! This is why attributes like a positive attitude, an enquiring mind and the ability to focus on what is important all have a major impact on your final result.

PLUSPOINTS

+ Resources help you to achieve your qualification. You will squander these unwittingly if you don't know what they are or how to use them properly.
+ Course information needs to be stored safely for future reference: course materials need to be filed promptly and accurately so that you can find them quickly.
+ You need your own set of key stationery items; you also need to know how to use any central facilities or resources such as the library, learning resource centres and your computer network.
+ People are often a key resource – school or college staff, work colleagues, members of your class, people who are experts in their field.
+ You can be your own best resource! Develop the skills you need to be able to work quickly and accurately and to get the most out of other people who can help you.

ACTION POINTS

✓ Under the same headings as in this section, list all the resources you need for your course and tick off those you currently have. Then decide how and when you can obtain anything vital that you lack.

✓ Check that you know how to access and use all the shared resources to which you have access at school or college.

✓ Pair up with someone on your course as a study buddy – and don't let them down!

✓ Test your own storage systems. How fast can you find notes or print-outs you made yesterday/last week/last month – and what condition are they in?

✓ Find out the IT policy at your school or college and make sure you abide by it.

STEP FIVE

UNDERSTAND YOUR ASSESSMENT

The key to doing really, really well on any BTEC National course is to understand exactly what you are expected to do in your assignments – and then to do it! It really is as simple as that. So why is it that some people go wrong?

Obviously you may worry that an assignment may be so difficult that it is beyond you. Actually this is highly unlikely to happen because all your assignments are based on topics you will have already covered thoroughly in class. Therefore, if you have attended regularly – and have clarified any queries or worries you have either in class or during your tutorials – this shouldn't happen. If you have had an unavoidable lengthy absence then you may need to review your progress with your tutor and decide how best to cope with the situation. Otherwise, you should note that the main problems with assignments are usually due to far more mundane pitfalls – such as:

✗ not reading the instructions or the assignment brief properly

✗ not understanding what you are supposed to do

✗ only doing part of the task or answering part of a question

✗ skimping the preparation, the research or the whole thing

✗ not communicating your ideas clearly

✗ guessing answers rather than researching properly

✗ padding out answers with irrelevant information

✗ leaving the work until the last minute and then doing it in a rush

✗ ignoring advice and feedback your tutor has given you.

You can avoid all of these traps by following the guidelines below so that you know exactly what you are doing, prepare well and produce your best work.

The assignment 'brief'

The word 'brief' is just another way of saying 'instructions'. Often, though, a 'brief' (despite its name!) may be rather longer. The brief sets the context for the work, defines what evidence you will need to produce and matches the grading criteria to the tasks. It will also give you a schedule for completing the tasks. For example, a brief may include details of a case study you have to read; research you have to carry out or a task you have to do, as well as questions you have to answer. Or it may give you details about a project or group presentation you have to prepare. The type of assignments you receive will depend partly upon the vocational area you are studying, but you can expect some to be in the form of written assignments. Others are likely to be more practical or project-based, especially if you are doing a very practical subject such as Art and Design, Performing Arts or Sport. You may also be assessed in the workplace. For example, this is a course requirement if you are studying Children's Care, Learning and Development.

The assignment brief may also include the **learning outcomes** to which it relates. These tell you the purpose of the assessment and the knowledge you need to demonstrate to obtain a required grade. If your brief doesn't list the learning outcomes, then you should check this information against the unit specification to see the exact knowledge you need to demonstrate.

The grade(s) you can obtain will also be stated on the assignment brief. Sometimes an assignment will focus on just one grade. Others may give you the opportunity to develop or extend your work to progress to a higher grade. This is often dependent upon submitting acceptable work at the previous grade first. You will see examples of this in the Marked Assignment section of this Study Guide on page 95.

The brief will also tell you if you have to do part of the work as a member of a group. In this case, you must identify your own contribution. You may also be expected to take part in a **peer review**, where you all give feedback on the contribution of one another. Remember that you should do this as objectively and professionally as possible – not just praise everyone madly in the hope that they will do the same for you! In any assignment where there is a group contribution, there is virtually always an individual component, so that your individual grade can be assessed accurately.

Finally, your assignment brief should state the final deadline for handing in the work as well as any interim review dates when you can discuss your progress and ideas with your tutor. These are very important dates indeed and should be entered immediately into your diary or planner. You should schedule your work around these dates so that you have made a start by the first date. This will then enable you to note any queries or significant issues you want to discuss. Otherwise you will waste a valuable opportunity to obtain useful feedback on your progress. Remember, too, to take a notebook to any review meetings so that you can write down the guidance you are given.

Your school or college rules and regulations

Your school or college will have a number of policies and guidelines about assignments and assessment. These will deal with issues such as:

- The procedure you must follow if you have a serious personal problem so cannot meet the deadline date and need an extension.
- Any penalties for missing a deadline date without any good reason.
- The penalties for copying someone else's work (**plagiarism**). These will be severe so make sure that you never share your work (including your CDs) with anyone else and don't ask to borrow theirs.
- The procedure to follow if you are unhappy with the final grade you receive.

Even though it is unlikely that you will ever need to use any of these policies, it is sensible to know they exist, and what they say, just as a safeguard.

Understanding the question or task

There are two aspects to a question or task that need attention. The first are the *command words*, which are explained below. The second are the *presentation instructions*, so that if you are asked to produce a table or graph or report then you do exactly that – and don't write a list or an essay instead!

Command words are used to specify how a question must be answered, eg 'explain', 'describe', 'analyse', 'evaluate'. These words relate to the type of answer required. So whereas you may be asked to 'describe' something at Pass level, you will need to do more (such as 'analyse' or 'evaluate') to achieve Merit or Distinction grade.

Many students fail to get a higher grade because they do not realise the difference between these words. They simply don't know *how* to analyse or evaluate, so give an explanation instead. Just adding to a list or giving a few more details will never give you a higher grade – instead you need to change your whole approach to the answer.

The **grading grid** for each unit of your course gives you the command words, so that you can find out exactly what you have to do in each unit, to obtain a Pass, Merit and Distinction. The following charts show you what is usually required when you see a particular command word. You can use this, and the assessed assignments on pages 95–142, to see the difference between the types of answers required for each grade. (The assignments your centre gives you will be specially written to ensure you have the opportunity to achieve all the possible grades.) Remember, though, that these are just examples to guide you. The exact response will often depend upon the way a question is worded, so if you have any doubts at all check with your tutor before you start work.

There are two other important points to note:

- Sometimes the same command word may be repeated for different grades – such as 'create' or 'explain'. In this case the *complexity* or *range* of the task itself increases at the higher grades – as you will see if you read the grading grid for the unit.
- Command words can also vary depending upon your vocational area. If you are studying Performing Arts or Art and Design you will probably find several command words that an Engineer or IT Practitioner would not – and vice versa!

To obtain a Pass grade

To achieve this grade you must usually demonstrate that you understand the important facts relating to a topic and can state these clearly and concisely.

Command word	What this means
Create (or produce)	Make, invent or construct an item.
Describe	Give a clear, straightforward description that includes all the main points and links these together logically.
Define	Clearly explain what a particular term means and give an example, if appropriate, to show what you mean.
Explain . . . how/why	Set out in detail the meaning of something, with reasons. It is often helpful to give an example of what you mean. Start with the topic then give the 'how' or 'why'.
Identify	Distinguish and state the main features or basic facts relating to a topic.
Interpret	Define or explain the meaning of something.
Illustrate	Give examples to show what you mean.
List	Provide the information required in a list rather than in continuous writing.
Outline	Write a clear description that includes all the main points but avoid going into too much detail.
Plan (or devise)	Work out and explain how you would carry out a task or activity.
Select (and present) information	Identify relevant information to support the argument you are making and communicate this in an appropriate way.
State	Write a clear and full account.
Undertake	Carry out a specific activity.
Examples: **Identify** the main features on a digital camera. **Describe** your usual lifestyle. **Outline** the steps to take to carry out research for an assignment.	

To obtain a Merit grade

To obtain this grade you must prove that you can apply your knowledge in a specific way.

Command word	What this means
Analyse	Identify separate factors, say how they are related and how each one relates to the topic.
Classify	Sort your information into appropriate categories before presenting or explaining it.
Compare and contrast	Identify the main factors that apply in two or more situations and explain the similarities and differences or advantages and disadvantages.
Demonstrate	Provide several relevant examples or appropriate evidence which support the arguments you are making. In some vocational areas this may also mean giving a practical performance.
Discuss	Provide a thoughtful and logical argument to support the case you are making.
Explain (in detail)	Provide details and give reasons and/or evidence to clearly support the argument you are making.
Implement	Put into practice or operation. You may also have to interpret or justify the effect or result.
Interpret	Understand and explain an effect or result.
Justify	Give appropriate reasons to support your opinion or views and show how you arrived at these conclusions.
Relate/report	Give a full account of, with reasons.
Research	Carry out a full investigation.
Specify	Provide full details and descriptions of selected items or activities.
Examples: **Compare and contrast** the performance of two different digital cameras. **Justify** your usual lifestyle. **Explain in detail** the steps to take to research an assignment.	

To obtain a Distinction grade

To obtain this grade you must prove that you can make a reasoned judgement based on appropriate evidence.

Command word	What this means
Analyse	Identify the key factors, show how they are linked and explain the importance and relevance of each.
Assess	Give careful consideration to all the factors or events that apply and identify which are the most important and relevant with reasons for your views.
Comprehensively explain	Give a very detailed explanation that covers all the relevant points and give reasons for your views or actions.
Comment critically	Give your view after you have considered all the evidence, particularly the importance of both the relevant positive and negative aspects.
Evaluate	Review the information and then bring it together to form a conclusion. Give evidence to support each of your views or statements.
Evaluate critically	Review the information to decide the degree to which something is true, important or valuable. Then assess possible alternatives taking into account their strengths and weaknesses if they were applied instead. Then give a precise and detailed account to explain your opinion.
Summarise	Identify review the main, relevant factors and/or arguments so that these are explained in a clear and concise manner.
Examples: **Assess** ten features commonly found on a digital camera. **Evaluate critically** your usual lifestyle. **Analyse** your own ability to carry out effective research for an assignment.	

Responding positively

This is often the most important attribute of all! If you believe that assignments give you the opportunity to demonstrate what you know and how you can apply it *and* positively respond to the challenge by being determined to give it your best shot, then you will do far better than someone who is defeated before they start.

It obviously helps, too, if you are well organised and have confidence in your own abilities – which is what the next section is all about!

PLUSPOINTS

+ Many mistakes in assignments are through errors that can easily be avoided such as not reading the instructions properly or doing only part of the task that was set!
+ Always read the assignment brief very carefully indeed. Check that you understand exactly what you have to do and the learning outcomes you must demonstrate.
+ Make a note of the deadline for an assignment and any interim review dates on your planner. Schedule work around these dates so that you can make the most of reviews with your tutor.
+ Make sure you know about school or college policies relating to assessment, such as how to obtain an extension or query a final grade.
+ For every assignment, make sure you understand the command words, which tell you how to answer the question, and the presentation instructions, which say what you must produce.
+ Command words are shown in the grading grid for each unit of your qualification. Expect command words and/or the complexity of a task to be different at higher grades, because you have to demonstrate higher-level skills.

ACTION POINTS

✓ Discuss with your tutor the format (style) of assignments you are likely to receive on your course, eg assignments, projects, or practical work where you are observed.

✓ Check the format of the assignments in the Assessed Assignments section of this book. Look at the type of work students did to gain a Pass and then look at the difference in the Merit answers. Read the tutor's comments carefully and ask your own tutor if there is anything you do not understand.

✓ Check out all the policies and guidelines at your school or college that relate to assessment and make sure you understand them.

✓ Check out the grading grid for the units you are currently studying and identify the command words for each grade. Then check you understand what they mean using the explanations above. If there are any words that are not included, ask your tutor to explain the meanings and what you would be required to do.

STEP SIX

SHARPEN YOUR SKILLS

To do your best in any assignment you need a number of skills. Some of these may be vocationally specific, or professional, skills that you are learning as part of your course – such as acting or dancing if you are taking a Performing Arts course or, perhaps, football if you are following a Sports course. Others, though, are broader skills that will help you to do well in assignments no matter what subjects or topics you are studying – such as communicating clearly and cooperating with others.

Some of these skills you will have already and in some areas you may be extremely proficient. Knowing where your weaknesses lie, though, and doing something about them has many benefits. You will work more quickly, more accurately *and* have increased confidence in your own abilities. As an extra bonus, all these skills also make you more effective at work – so there really is no excuse for not giving yourself a quick skills check and then remedying any problem areas.

This section contains hints and tips to help you check out and improve each of the following areas:

- Your numeracy skills
- Keyboarding and document preparation
- Your IT skills
- Your written communication skills
- Working with others
- Researching information
- Making a presentation
- Problem solving and staying focused

Improving your numeracy skills

Some people have the idea that they can ignore numeracy because this skill isn't relevant to their vocational area – such as Art and Design or Children's Care, Learning and Development. If this is how you think then you are wrong! Numeracy is a life skill that everyone needs, so if you can't carry out basic calculations accurately then you will have problems, often when you least expect them.

Numeracy is a life skill

Fortunately there are several things you can do to remedy this situation:

- Practise basic calculations in your head and then check them on a calculator.
- Ask your tutor if there are any essential calculations which give you difficulties.
- Use your onscreen calculator (or a spreadsheet package) to do calculations for you when you are using your computer.
- Try your hand at Sudoku puzzles – either on paper or by using a software package or online at sites such as www.websudoku.com/.
- Investigate puzzle sites and brain training software, such as http://school.discovery.com/brainboosters/ and Dr Kawashima's Brain Training by Nintendo.
- Check out online sites such as www.bbc.co.uk/skillswise/ and www.bbc.co.uk/schools/ks3bitesize/maths/number/index.shtml to improve your skills.

Keyboarding and document preparation

- Think seriously about learning to touch type to save hours of time! Your school or college may have a workshop you can join or you can learn online such as by downloading a free program at www.sense-lang.org/typing/ or practising on sites such as www.computerlab.kids.new.net/keyboarding.htm.
- Obtain correct examples of document formats you will have to use, such as a report or summary. Your tutor may provide you with these or you can find examples in many communication textbooks.
- Proofread work you produce on a computer *carefully*. Remember that your spell checker will not pick up every mistake you make, such as a mistyped word that makes another word (eg form/from; sheer/shear)

and grammar checkers, too, are not without their problems! This means you still have to read your work through yourself. If possible, let your work go 'cold' before you do this so that you read it afresh and don't make assumptions about what you have written. Then read word by word to make sure it still makes sense and there are no silly mistakes, such as missing or duplicated words.

- Make sure your work looks professional by using an appropriate typeface and font size as well as suitable margins.
- Print out your work carefully and store it neatly, so it looks in pristine condition when you hand it in.

Your IT skills

- Check that you can use the main features of all the software packages that you will need to produce your assignments, such as Word, Excel and PowerPoint.
- Adopt a good search engine, such as Google, and learn to use it properly. Many have online tutorials such as www.googleguide.com.
- Develop your IT skills to enable you to enhance your assignments appropriately. For example, this may include learning how to import and export text and artwork from one package to another; taking digital photographs and inserting them into your work and/or creating drawings or diagrams by using appropriate software for your course.

Your written communication skills

A poor vocabulary will reduce your ability to explain yourself clearly; work peppered with spelling or punctuation errors looks unprofessional.

- Read more. This introduces you to new words and familiarises you over and over again with the correct way to spell words.
- Look up words you don't understand in a dictionary and then try to use them yourself in conversation.
- Use the Thesaurus in Word to find alternatives to words you find yourself regularly repeating, to add variety to your work.
- *Never* use words you don't understand in the hope that they sound impressive!
- Do crosswords to improve your word power and spelling.
- Resolve to master punctuation – especially apostrophes – either by using an online programme or working your way through the relevant section of a communication textbook that you like.
- Check out online sites such as www.bbc.co.uk/skillswise/ and www.bbc.co.uk/schools/gcsebitesize/english/ as well as puzzle sites with communication questions such as http://school.discovery.com/brainboosters/.

Working with others

In your private life you can choose who you want to be with and how you respond to them. At work you cannot do that – you are paid to be professional and this means working alongside a wide variety of people, some of whom you may like and some of whom you may not!

The same applies at school or college. By the time you have reached BTEC National level you will be expected to have outgrown wanting to work with your best friends on every project! You may not be very keen on everyone who is in the same team as you, but – at the very least – you can be pleasant, cooperative and helpful. In a large group this isn't normally too difficult. You may find it much harder if you have to partner someone who has very different ideas and ways of working to you.

In this case it may help if you:

- Realise that everyone is different and that your ways of working may not always be the best!
- Are prepared to listen and contribute to a discussion (positively) in equal amounts. Make sure, too, that you encourage the quiet members of the group to speak up by asking them what their views are. The ability to draw other people into the discussion is an important and valuable skill to learn.
- Write down what you have said you will do, so that you don't forget anything.
- Are prepared to do your fair share of the work.
- Discuss options and alternatives with people – don't give them orders or meekly accept instructions and then resent it afterwards.
- Don't expect other people to do what you wouldn't be prepared to do.
- Are sensitive to other people's feelings and remember that they may have personal problems or issues that affect their behaviour.
- *Always* keep your promises and never let anyone down when they are depending upon you.
- Don't flounce around or lose your temper if things get tough. Instead take a break while you cool down. Then sit down and discuss the issues that are annoying you.
- Help other people to reach a compromise when necessary, by acting as peacemaker.

Researching information

Poor researchers either cannot find what they want or find too much – and then drown in a pile of papers. If you find yourself drifting aimlessly around a library when you want information or printing out dozens of pages for no apparent purpose, then this section is for you!

- Always check *exactly* what it is you need to find and how much detail is needed. Write down a few key words to keep yourself focused.
- Discipline yourself to ignore anything that is irrelevant – from books with interesting titles to websites which sound tempting but have little to do with your topic or key words.
- Remember that you could theoretically research information forever! So at some time you have to call a halt. Learning when to do this is another skill, but you can learn this by writing out a schedule which clearly states when you have to stop looking and start sorting out your information and writing about it!

- In a library, check you know how the books are stored and what other types of media are available. If you can't find what you are looking for then ask the librarian for help. Checking the index in a book is the quickest way to find out whether it contains information related to your key words. Put it back if it doesn't or if you can't understand it. If you find three or four books and/or journals that contain what you need then that is usually enough.
- Online use a good search engine and use the summary of the search results to check out the best sites. Force yourself to check out sites beyond page one of the search results! When you enter a site investigate it carefully – use the site map if necessary. It isn't always easy to find exactly what you want. Bookmark sites you find helpful and will want to use again and only take print-outs when the information is closely related to your key words.
- Talk to people who can help you (see also Step 4 – Utilise all your resources) and prepare in advance by thinking about the best questions to ask. Always explain why you want the information and don't expect anyone to tell you anything that is confidential or sensitive – such as personal information or financial details. Always write clear notes so that you remember what you have been told, by whom and when. If you are wise you will also note down their contact details so that you can contact them again if you think of anything later. If you remember to be courteous and thank them for their help, this shouldn't be a problem.
- Store all your precious information carefully and neatly in a labelled folder so that you can find it easily. Then, when you are ready to start work, reread it and extract that which is most closely related to your key words and the task you are doing.
- Make sure you state the source of all the information you quote by including the name of the author or the web address, either in the text or as part of a bibliography at the end. Your school or college will have a help sheet which will tell you exactly how to do this.

Making a presentation

This involves several skills – which is why it is such a popular way of finding out what students can do! It will test your ability to work in a team, speak in public and use IT (normally PowerPoint) – as well as your nerves. It is therefore excellent practice for many of the tasks you will have to do when you are at work – from attending an interview to talking to an important client.

You will be less nervous if you have prepared well and have rehearsed your role beforehand. You will produce a better, more professional presentation if you take note of the following points.

- If you are working as a team, work out everyone's strengths and weaknesses and divide up the work (fairly) taking these into account. Work out, too, how long each person should speak and who would be the best as the 'leader' who introduces each person and then summarises everything at the end.

PLUSPOINTS

+ Poor numeracy skills can let you down in your assignments and at work. Work at improving these if you regularly struggle with even simple calculations.
+ Good keyboarding, document production and IT skills can save you hours of time and mean that your work is of a far more professional standard. Improve any of these areas which are letting you down.
+ Your written communication skills will be tested in many assignments. Work at improving areas of weakness, such as spelling, punctuation or vocabulary.
+ You will be expected to work cooperatively with other people both at work and during many assignments. Be sensitive to other people's feelings, not just your own, and always be prepared to do your fair share of the work and help other people when you can.
+ To research effectively you need to know exactly what you are trying to find and where to look. This means understanding how reference media is stored in your library as well as how to search online. Good organisation skills also help so that you store important information carefully and can find it later. And never forget to include your sources in a bibliography.
+ Making a presentation requires several skills and may be nerve-racking at first. You will reduce your problems if you prepare well, are not too ambitious and have several run-throughs beforehand. Remember to speak clearly and a little more slowly than normal and smile from time to time!

ACTION POINTS

✓ Test both your numeracy and literacy skills at http://www.move-on.org.uk/testyourskills.asp# to check your current level. You don't need to register on the site if you click to do the 'mini-test' instead. If either need improvement, get help at http://www.bbc.co.uk/keyskills/it/1.shtml.

✓ Do the following two tasks with a partner to jerk your brain into action!

- Each write down 36 simple calculations in a list, eg 8 x 6, 19 – 8, 14 + 6. Then exchange lists. See who can answer the most correctly in the shortest time.
- Each write down 30 short random words (no more than 8 letters), eg cave, table, happily. Exchange lists. You each have three minutes to try to remember as many words as possible. Then hand back the list and write down all those you can recall. See who can remember the most.

✓ Assess your own keyboarding, proof-reading, document production, written communication and IT skills. Then find out if your tutors agree with you!

✓ List ten traits in other people that drive you mad. Then, for each one, suggest what you could do to cope with the problem (or solve it) rather than make a fuss. Compare your ideas with other members of your group.

✓ Take a note of all feedback you receive from your tutors, especially in relation to working with other people, researching and giving presentations. In each case focus on their suggestions and ideas so that you continually improve your skills throughout the course.

- Don't be over-ambitious. Take account of your time-scale, resources and the skills of the team. Remember that a simple, clear presentation is often more professional than an over-elaborate or complicated one where half the visual aids don't work properly!
- If you are using PowerPoint try to avoid preparing every slide with bullet points! For variety, include some artwork and vary the designs. Remember that you should *never* just read your slides to the audience! Instead prepare notes that you can print out that will enable you to enhance and extend what the audience is reading.

- Your preparations should also include checking the venue and time; deciding what to wear and getting it ready; preparing, checking and printing any handouts; deciding what questions might be asked and how to answer these.
- Have several run-throughs beforehand and check your timings. Check, too, that you can be heard clearly. This means lifting up your head and 'speaking' to the back of the room a little more slowly and loudly than you normally do.
- On the day, arrive in plenty of time so that you aren't rushed or stressed. Remember that taking deep breaths helps to calm your nerves.
- Start by introducing yourself clearly and smile at the audience. If it helps, find a friendly face and pretend you are just talking to that person.
- Answer any questions honestly and don't exaggerate, guess or waffle. If you don't know the answer then say so!
- If you are giving the presentation in a team, help out someone else who is struggling with a question if you know the answer.
- Don't get annoyed or upset if you get any negative feedback afterwards. Instead take note so that you can concentrate on improving your own performance next time. And don't focus on one or two criticisms and ignore all the praise you received! Building on the good and minimising the bad is how everyone improves in life!

STEP SEVEN

MAXIMISE YOUR OPPORTUNITIES AND MANAGE YOUR PROBLEMS

Like most things in life, you may have a few ups and downs on your course – particularly if you are studying over quite a long time, such as one or two years. Sometimes everything will be marvellous – you are enjoying all the units, you are up-to-date with your work, you are finding the subjects interesting and having no problems with any of your research tasks. At other times you may struggle a little more. You may find one or two topics rather tedious, or there may be distractions or worries in your personal life that you have to cope with. You may struggle to concentrate on the work and do your best.

Rather than just suffering in silence or gritting your teeth if things go a bit awry it is sensible if you have an action plan to help you cope. Equally, rather than just accepting good opportunities for additional experiences or learning, it is also wise to plan how to make the best of these. This section will show you how to do this.

Making the most of your opportunities

The following are examples of opportunities to find out more about information relevant to your course or to try putting some of your skills into practice.

- **External visits** You may go out of college on visits to different places or organisations. These are not days off – there is a reason for making each trip. Prepare in advance by reading around relevant topics and make notes of useful information whilst you are there. Then write (or type) it up neatly as soon as you can and file it where you can find it again!
- **Visiting speakers** Again, people are asked to talk to your group for a purpose. You are likely to be asked to contribute towards questions that may be asked – which may be submitted in advance so that the speaker is clear on the topics you are studying. Think carefully about information that you would find helpful so that you can ask one or two relevant and useful questions. Take notes whilst the speaker is addressing your group, unless someone is recording the session. Be prepared to thank the speaker on behalf of your group if you are asked to do so.
- **Professional contacts** These will be the people you meet on work experience doing the real job that one day you hope to do. Make the most of meeting these people to find out about the vocational area of your choice.
- **Work experience** If you need to undertake practical work for any particular units of your BTEC National qualification, and if you are studying full-time, then your tutor will organise a work experience placement for you and talk to you about the evidence you need to obtain. You may also be issued with a special log book or diary in which to record your experiences. Before you start your placement, check that you are clear about all the details, such as the time you will start and leave, the name of your supervisor, what you should wear and what you should do if you are ill during the placement and cannot attend. Read and reread the units to which your evidence will apply and make sure you understand the grading criteria and what you need to obtain. Then make a note of appropriate headings to record your information. Try to make time to write up your notes, log book and/or diary every night, whilst your experiences are fresh in your mind.
- **In your own workplace** You may be studying your BTEC National qualification on a part-time basis and also have a full-time job in the same vocational area. Or you may be studying full-time and have a part-time job just to earn some money. In either case you should be alert to opportunities to find out more about topics that relate to your workplace, no matter how generally. For example, many BTEC courses include topics such as health and safety, teamwork, dealing with customers, IT security and communications – to name but a few. All these are topics that your employer will have had to address and finding out more about these will broaden your knowledge and help to give more depth to your assignment responses.
- **Television programmes, newspapers, Podcasts and other information sources.** No matter what vocational area you are studying, the media are likely to be an invaluable source of information. You should be alert to any news bulletins that relate to your studies as well as relevant information in more topical television programmes. For example, if you are studying Art and Design then you should make a particular effort to watch the *Culture Show* as well as programmes on artists, exhibitions

or other topics of interest. Business students should find inspiration by watching *Dragons Den*, *The Apprentice* and the *Money Programme* and Travel and Tourism students should watch holiday, travel and adventure programmes. If you are studying Media, Music and Performing Arts then you are spoiled for choice! Whatever your vocational choice, there will be television and radio programmes of special interest to you.

Remember that you can record television programmes to watch later if you prefer, and check out newspaper headlines online and from sites such as BBC news. The same applies to Podcasts. Of course, to know which information is relevant means that you must be familiar with the content of all the units you are studying, so it is useful to know what topics you will be learning about in the months to come, as well as the ones you are covering now. That way you can recognise useful opportunities when they arise.

The media are invaluable sources of information

Minimising problems

If you are fortunate, any problems you experience on your course will only be minor ones. For example, you may struggle to keep yourself motivated every single day and there may be times that you are having difficulty with a topic. Or you may be struggling to work with someone else in your team or to understand a particular tutor.

During induction you should have been told which tutor to talk to in this situation, and who to see if that person is absent or if you would prefer to see someone else. If you are having difficulties which are distracting you and affecting your work then it is sensible to ask to see your tutor promptly so that you can talk in confidence, rather than just trusting to luck everything will go right again. It is a rare student who is madly enthusiastic about every part of a course and all the other people on the course, so your tutor won't be surprised and will be able to give you useful guidance to help you stay on track.

If you are very unlucky, you may have a more serious personal problem to deal with. In this case it is important that you know the main sources of help in your school or college and how to access these.

- **Professional counselling** There may be a professional counselling service if you have a concern that you don't want to discuss with any teaching staff. If you book an appointment to see a counsellor then you can be certain that nothing you say will ever be mentioned to another member of staff without your permission.
- **Student complaint procedures** If you have a serious complaint to make then the first step is to talk to a tutor, but you should be aware of the formal student complaint procedures that exist if you cannot resolve the problem informally. Note that these are only used for serious issues, not for minor difficulties.
- **Student appeals procedures** If you cannot agree with a tutor about a final grade for an assignment then you need to check the grading criteria and ask the tutor to explain how the grade was awarded. If you are still unhappy then you should see your personal tutor. If you still disagree then you have the right to make a formal appeal.

- **Student disciplinary procedures** These exist so that all students who flout the rules in a school or college will be dealt with in the same way. Obviously it is wise to avoid getting into trouble at any time, but if you find yourself on the wrong side of the regulations do read the procedures carefully to see what could happen. Remember that being honest about what happened and making a swift apology is always the wisest course of action, rather than being devious or trying to blame someone else.
- **Serious illness** Whether this affects you or a close family member, it could severely affect your attendance. The sooner you discuss the problem with your tutor the better. This is because you will be missing notes and information from the first day you do not attend. Many students under-estimate the ability of their tutors to find inventive solutions in this type of situation – from sending notes by post to updating you electronically if you are well enough to cope with the work.

PLUSPOINTS

+ Some students miss out on opportunities to learn more about relevant topics. This may be because they haven't read the unit specifications, so don't know what topics they will be learning about in future; haven't prepared in advance or don't take advantage of occasions when they can listen to an expert and perhaps ask questions. Examples of these occasions include external visits, visiting speakers, work experience, being at work and watching television.
+ Many students encounter minor difficulties, especially if their course lasts a year or two. It is important to talk to your tutor, or another appropriate person, promptly if you have a worry that is affecting your work.
+ All schools and colleges have procedures for dealing with important issues and problems such as serious complaints, major illnesses, student appeals and disciplinary matters. It is important to know what these are.

ACTION POINTS

✓ List the type of opportunities available on your course for obtaining more information and talking to experts. Then check with your tutor to make sure you haven't missed out any.

✓ Check out the content of each unit you will be studying so that you know the main topics you have still to study.

✓ Identify the type of information you can find on television, in newspapers and in Podcasts that will be relevant to your studies.

✓ Check out your school or college documents and procedures to make sure that you know who to talk to in a crisis and who you can see if the first person is absent.

✓ Find out where you can read a copy of the main procedures in your school or college that might affect you if you have a serious problem. Then do so.

AND FINALLY . . .

Don't expect this Introduction to be of much use if you skim through it quickly and then put it to one side. Instead, refer to it whenever you need to remind yourself about something related to your course.

The same applies to the rest of this Student Guide. The Activities in the next section have been written to help you to demonstrate your understanding of many of the key topics contained in the core or specialist units you are studying. Your tutor may tell you to do these at certain times; otherwise there is nothing to stop you working through them yourself!

Similarly, the Assessed Assignments in the final section have been written to show you how your assignments may be worded. You can also see the type of response that will achieve a Pass, Merit and Distinction – as well as the type of response that won't! Read these carefully and if any comment or grade puzzles you, ask your tutor to explain it.

Then keep this guide in a safe place so that you can use it whenever you need to refresh your memory. That way, you will get the very best out of your course – and yourself!

GLOSSARY

Note: all words highlighted in bold in the text are defined in the glossary.

Accreditation of Prior Learning (APL)

APL is an assessment process that enables your previous achievements and experiences to count towards your qualification providing your evidence is authentic, current, relevant and sufficient.

Apprenticeships

Schemes that enable you to work and earn money at the same time as you gain further qualifications (an **NVQ** award and a technical certificate) and improve your key skills. Apprentices learn work-based skills relevant to their job role and their chosen industry. You can find out more at www.apprenticeships.org.uk/

Assessment methods

Methods, such as **assignments**, case studies and practical tasks, used to check that your work demonstrates the learning and understanding required for your qualification.

Assessor

The tutor who marks or assesses your work.

Assignment

A complex task or mini-project set to meet specific **grading criteria**.

Awarding body

The organisation which is responsible for devising, assessing and issuing qualifications. The awarding body for all BTEC qualifications is Edexcel.

Core units

On a BTEC National course these are the compulsory or mandatory units that all students must complete to gain the qualification. Some BTEC qualifications have an over-arching title, eg Engineering, but within Engineering you can choose different routes. In this case you will study both common core units that are common to all engineering qualifications and **specialist core unit(s)** which are specific to your chosen **pathway**.

Degrees

These are higher education qualifications which are offered by universities and colleges. Foundation degrees take two years to complete; honours degrees may take three years or longer. See also **Higher National Certificates and Diplomas**.

DfES

The Department for Education and Skills: this is the government department responsible for education issues. You can find out more at www.dfes.gov.uk

Distance learning

This enables you to learn and/or study for a qualification without attending an Edexcel centre although you would normally be supported by a member of staff who works there. You communicate with your tutor and/or the centre that organises the distance learning programme by post, telephone or electronically.

Educational Maintenance Award (EMA)

This is a means-tested award which provides eligible students under 19, who are studying a full-time course at school or college, with a cash sum of money every week. See http://www.dfes.gov.uk/financialhelp/ema/ for up-to-date details.

External verification

Formal checking by a representative of Edexcel of the way a BTEC course is delivered. This includes sampling various assessments to check content and grading.

Final major project

This is a major, individual piece of work that is designed to enable you to demonstrate you have achieved several learning outcomes for a BTEC National qualification in the creative or performing arts. Like all assessments, this is internally assessed.

Forbidden combinations

Qualifications or units that cannot be taken simultaneously because their content is too similar.

GLH

See **Guided Learning Hours** below

Grade

The rating (Pass, Merit or Distinction) given to the mark you have obtained which identifies the standard you have achieved.

Grade boundaries

The pre-set points at which the total points you have earned for different units converts to the overall grade(s) for your qualification.

Grading criteria

The standard you have to demonstrate to obtain a particular grade in the unit, in other words, what you have to prove you can do.

Grading domains

The main areas of learning which support the **learning outcomes**. On a BTEC National course these are: application of knowledge and understanding; development of practical and technical skills; personal development for occupational roles; application of generic and **key skills**. Generic skills are basic skills needed wherever you work, such as the ability to work cooperatively as a member of a team.

Grading grid

The table in each unit of your BTEC qualification specification that sets out the **grading criteria**.

Guided Learning Hours (GLH)

The approximate time taken to deliver a unit which includes the time taken for direct teaching, instruction and assessment and for you to carry out directed assignments or directed individual study. It does not include any time you spend on private study or researching an assignment. The GLH determines the size of the unit. At BTEC National level, units are either 30, 60, 90 or 120 guided learning hours. By looking at the number of GLH a unit takes, you can see the size of the unit and how long it is likely to take you to learn and understand the topics it contains.

Higher education (HE)

Post-secondary and post-further education, usually provided by universities and colleges.

Higher level skills

Skills such as evaluating or critically assessing complex information that are more difficult than lower level skills such as writing a description or making out a list. You must be able to demonstrate higher level skills to achieve a Distinction grade.

Higher National Certificates and Diplomas

Higher National Certificates and Diplomas are vocational qualifications offered at colleges around the country. Certificates are part-time and designed to be studied by people who are already in work; students can use their work experiences to build on their learning. Diplomas are full-time courses – although often students will spend a whole year on work experience part way through their Diploma. Higher Nationals are roughly equivalent to half a degree.

Indicative reading

Recommended books and journals whose content is both suitable and relevant for the unit.

Induction

A short programme of events at the start of a course designed to give you essential information and introduce you to your fellow students and tutors so that you can settle down as quickly and easily as possible.

Internal verification

The quality checks carried out by nominated tutor(s) at your school or college to ensure that all assignments are at the right level and cover appropriate learning outcomes. The checks also ensure that all **assessors** are marking work consistently and to the same standard.

Investors in People (IIP)

A national quality standard which sets a level of good practice for the training and development of people. Organisations must demonstrate their commitment to achieve the standard.

Key skills

The transferable, essential skills you need both at work and to run your own life successfully. They are: literacy, numeracy, IT, problem solving, working with others and self-management.

Learning outcomes

The knowledge and skills you must demonstrate to show that you have effectively learned a unit.

Learning support

Additional help that is available to all students in a school or college who have learning difficulties or other special needs. These include reasonable adjustments to help to reduce the effect of a disability or difficulty that would place a student at a substantial disadvantage in an assessment situation.

Levels of study

The depth, breadth and complexity of knowledge, understanding and skills required to achieve a qualification determines its level. Level 2 is broadly equivalent to GCSE level (grades A*-C) and level 3 equates to GCE level. As you successfully achieve one level, you can then progress on to the next. BTEC qualifications are offered at Entry level, then levels 1, 2, 3, 4 and 5.

Learning and Skills Council (LSC)

The government body responsible for planning and funding education and training for everyone aged over 16 in England - except university students. You can find out more at www.lsc.gov.uk

Local Education Authority (LEA)

The local government body responsible for providing education for students of compulsory school age in your area.

Mentor

A more experienced person who will guide and counsel you if you have a problem or difficulty.

Mode of delivery

The way in which a qualification is offered to students, eg part-time, full-time, as a short course or by **distance learning**.

National Occupational Standard (NOS)

These are statements of the skills, knowledge and understanding you need to develop to be competent at a particular job. These are drawn up by the **Sector Skills Councils**.

National Qualification Framework (NQF)

The framework into which all accredited qualifications in the UK are placed. Each is awarded a level based on their difficulty which ensures that all those at the same level are of the same standard. (See also **levels of study**).

National Vocational Qualification (NVQ)

Qualifications which concentrate upon the practical skills and knowledge required to do a job competently. They are usually assessed in the workplace and range from level 1 (the lowest) to level 5 (the highest).

Nested qualifications

Qualifications which have 'common' units, so that students can easily progress from one to another by adding on more units, such as the BTEC Award, BTEC Certificate and BTEC Diploma.

Pathway

All BTEC National qualifications are comprised of a small number of core units and a larger number of specialist units. These specialist units are grouped into different combinations to provide alternative pathways to achieving the qualification, linked to different career preferences.

Peer review

An occasion when you give feedback on the performance of other members in your team and they, in turn, comment on your performance.

Plagiarism

The practice of copying someone else's work and passing it off as your own. *This is strictly forbidden on all courses.*

Portfolio

A collection of work compiled by a student, usually as evidence of learning to produce for an **assessor**.

Professional body

An organisation that exists to promote or support a particular profession, such as the Law Society and the Royal Institute of British Architects.

Professional development and training

Activities that you can undertake, relevant to your job, that will increase and/or update your knowledge and skills.

Project

A comprehensive piece of work which normally involves original research and investigation either by an individual or a team. The findings and results may be presented in writing and summarised in a presentation.

Qualifications and Curriculum Authority (QCA)

The public body, sponsored by the **DfES**, responsible for maintaining and developing the national curriculum and associated assessments, tests and examinations. It also accredits and monitors qualifications in colleges and at work. You can find out more at www.qca.gov.uk

Quality assurance

In education, this is the process of continually checking that a course of study is meeting the specific requirements set down by the awarding body.

Sector Skills Councils (SSCs)

The 25 employer-led, independent organisations that are responsible for improving workforce skills in the UK by identifying skill gaps and improving learning in the workplace. Each council covers a different type of industry and develops its **National Occupational Standards**.

Semester

Many universities and colleges divide their academic year into two halves or semesters, one from September to January and one from February to July.

Seminar

A learning event between a group of students and a tutor. This may be student-led, following research into a topic which has been introduced earlier.

Specialist core units

See under **Core units**.

Study buddy

A person in your group or class who takes notes for you and keeps you informed of important developments if you are absent. You do the same in return.

Time-constrained assignment

An assessment you must complete within a fixed time limit.

Tutorial

An individual or small group meeting with your tutor at which you can discuss the work you are currently doing and other more general course issues. At an individual tutorial your progress on the course will be discussed and you can also raise any concerns or personal worries you have.

The University and Colleges Admissions Service (UCAS)

The central organisation which processes all applications for higher education courses. You pronounce this 'You-Cass'.

UCAS points

The number of points allocated by **UCAS** for the qualifications you have obtained. **HE** institutions specify how many points you need to be accepted on the courses they offer. You can find out more at www.ucas.com

Unit abstract

The summary at the start of each BTEC unit that tells you what the unit is about.

Unit content

Details about the topics covered by the unit and the knowledge and skills you need to complete it.

Unit points

The number of points you have gained when you complete a unit. These depend upon the grade you achieve (Pass, Merit or Distinction) and the size of the unit as determined by its **guided learning hours**.

Vocational qualification

A qualification which is designed to develop the specific knowledge and understanding relevant to a chosen area of work.

Work experience

Any time you spend on an employer's premises when you carry out work-based tasks as an employee but also learn about the enterprise and develop your skills and knowledge.

ACTIVITIES

This unit focuses on grading criteria P1, P2, P3; M1, M2, M3; D1, D2 and D3.

Learning outcomes

1 Understand the purposes of research in the media industries
2 Be able to apply a range of research methods and techniques
3 Be able to present results of research

Content

1) Understand the purposes of research in the media industries

Market research: audience data; audience awareness; product reach; audience profiling; consumer behaviour; consumer attitudes; competitor analysis; advertising placement; advertising effects

Production research: content; resources, eg personnel, talent, finance, suppliers, facilities, locations, logistical support; costs; viability; placement, eg publication, broadcast, webcast, podcast; audience; competition

2) Be able to apply a range of research methods and techniques

Resource procedures: search methods (subject indexes, search engines, file transfer protocol); catalogues; loan methods; reservations; borrowing materials; reference only sources; interlibrary loans

Types of research: quantitative research, eg programme ratings, readership circulation figures, hits on a website, box office figures, sales of CDs and DVDs; qualitative research, eg film reviews, game reviews, fanzine websites, attitudes to media products, responses to news coverage, responses to advertising campaigns, discussion of reality television

Primary sources: interview (face-to-face, telephone, email); bias in interviewing contexts (uniformity of questioning, interpersonal dynamics, interference, influence); observations; questionnaires; surveys; focus groups; audience panels; meetings; self-generated, eg own video, audio or photographic records of events

Secondary sources: books; journals; reference-based books and directories; periodicals; newspapers; film archives; photo libraries; worldwide web; CD Rom databases; audio material; interviews; published statistics (ratings, circulation figures, government statistics); data gathering agencies, eg BARB (Broadcasters' Audience Research Board), RAJAR (Radio Joint Audience Research Ltd), ABC

Consumer categorisation: socio-economic classification; geodemographic classification; psychographic classification; ethnographic classification; age; gender; sexual orientation; occupational groups; educational background

Interpreting results: collate; evaluate; summarise

3) Be able to present results of research

Techniques: written (word processed, reports, reviews); oral (individual presentation, group presentation, PowerPoint, overhead transparencies, video and audio illustration, multimedia, video diary, audio diary); graphic aids (graphs, pie charts, bar charts); style, eg formal, informal

Content: procedures; research data; research findings; conclusions and proposals

Quotation and reference: bibliography styles, eg Modern Languages Association (MLA), Harvard, American Psychological Association (APA); citation; footnotes; acknowledgements; credits; appendices

Copyright: material, eg print, film, video, audio, photographs, published letters; photocopying; quotation and citation; disclaimers

Grading criteria

P1 describe purposes of research in the media industries expressing ideas with sufficient clarity to communicate them and with some appropriate use of subject terminology

This means that you will be able to outline the main purposes of research covering both market research and production research. You will be able to communicate simple ideas about research effectively.

P2 apply research methods and techniques with some assistance

This means that you should be able to use all the research methods listed in Learning Outcome 2 to help you to make a media product, but you will probably need help from your teacher.

P3 present results, expressing ideas with sufficient clarity to communicate them and with some appropriate use of subject terminology

This means that the results you produce, which might be lists of information, should be presented clearly enough for your teacher/tutor to understand them and that you should know and use some media terms correctly.

M1 explain purposes of research in the media industries with well-chosen examples expressing ideas with clarity and with generally appropriate use of subject terminology

You will be able to talk about why and how research is completed in the media industries. You will be able to communicate fairly complex ideas.

M2 apply research methods and techniques competently with only occasional assistance

For this grade you should be able to use all the research methods listed in Learning Outcome 2 and rarely ask for help from your teacher.

M3 present results competently, expressing ideas with clarity and with generally appropriate use of subject terminology

To get the merit you must go one stage further and give reasons for your results, explaining your ideas clearly and using mainly media vocabulary to do so.

D1 fully explain purposes of research in the media industries with supporting arguments and elucidated examples expressing ideas fluently and using subject terminology correctly

You will be able to explain your ideas extremely well, using appropriate media language to explain complex ideas.

D2 apply research methods and techniques to near-professional standards, working independently to professional expectations

To get a distinction you need to be able to use all the research methods in Learning Outcome 2 without asking for help from your teacher, and to be able to do it almost as well as a professional researcher.

D3 present results to near-professional standards, expressing ideas fluently and using subject terminology correctly

For a distinction you need to present your results as if working with a real client. You should use media language accurately and fluently and present your ideas with confidence and fluency.

UNDERSTAND THE PURPOSES OF RESEARCH IN THE MEDIA INDUSTRIES

This section focuses on grading criteria P1, M1 and D1 from Unit 1 – Research techniques for the Media Industries. Each of the activities will help you to learn more about why we need to carry out research when making media products.

ACTIVITY 1

MARKET RESEARCH

A key part of all successful media production work is research. The content of any media product, whether factual or fiction, must be believable and appropriate to the audience. Content research for media products is necessary to establish a valid, current, reliable and truthful basis upon which to make a product.

All media products must be sold to a target audience, or a consumer, either directly through the retail system, or indirectly through the tax system or through advertising. Producers need to be sure that they are targeting the correct consumer or audience and this requires audience or market research.

Research is a process that is undertaken through a series of tasks, the results of which provide a basis for a production.

By completing these tasks you obtain results, findings or information that inform you whether your audience ideas are valid and whether the product that you intend to make is going to be fit for its intended audience.

The research process, whether for audience or content, starts by finding data from a range of sources. Data is then validated and all unreliable data discarded. Reliable data is sorted and stored and analysed to establish its meaning and the consequences for the media product and its audience. The findings of analysis are then worked into the product, or in the case of audience research a match is established between the product and a target audience.

TV Viewing 22 April 2007						
Channel	Average Daily Reach		Weekly Reach		Average Weekly Viewing	Share
	000s	%	000s	%	Hrs: Mins per person	%
ALL/ANY TV	41,718	74.3	52,937	94.2	23:30	100.0
BBC1 (incl. Breakfast News)	27,982	49.8	46,933	83.6	5:07	21.8
BBC2	15,753	28.0	37,221	66.3	2:01	8.6
TOTAL BBC1/BBC2	31,175	55.5	48,461	86.3	7:08	30.4
ITV (incl. GMTV)	22,432	39.9	42,385	75.5	4:22	18.6
CHANNEL 4/S4C	15,846	28.2	38,082	67.8	2:00	8.5
Five	9,172	16.3	26,498	47.2	1:15	5.3
TOTAL/ANY COMM. TERR. TV	30,077	53.5	48,310	86.0	7:37	32.4
Other Viewing	25,561	45.5	39,825	70.9	8:45	37.2

TV Viewing 21 May 2002				
Channel	Average Daily Reach	Weekly Reach	Average Weekly Viewing	Share
	%	%	Hrs: Mins per person	%
ALL/ANY TV	76.1	91.8	22:55	100.0
BBC1 (incl. Breakfast News)	54.6	84.0	5:47	25.3
BBC2	35.3	73.3	2:25	10.5
TOTAL BBC1/BBC2	60.9	86.7	8:12	35.8
ITV (incl. GMTV)	49.7	82.4	5:42	24.9
CHANNEL 4/S4C	32.2	71.6	2:11	9.5
Five	20.8	50.2	1:31	6.6
TOTAL/ANY COMM. TERR. TV	60.8	87.7	9:25	41.1
Other Viewing	29.1	42.4	5:18	23.1

TV Viewing 03 May 1998				
Channel	Average Daily Reach	Weekly Reach	Average Weekly Viewing	Share
	%	%	Hrs: Mins per person	%
ALL/ANY TV	80.0	95.6	23:57	100.0
BBC1 (incl. Breakfast News)	62.2	91.5	6:41	27.9
BBC2	42.1	81.1	3:24	14.2
TOTAL BBC1/BBC2	68.9	93.2	10:05	42.1
ITV (incl. GMTV)	60.7	90.0	7:26	31.0
CHANNEL 4/S4C	36.9	78.2	2:29	10.4
Five	14.8	39.2	0:56	3.9
TOTAL/ANY COMM. TERR. TV	67.8	92.3	10:51	45.3
Other Viewing	19.0	28.6	3:01	12.6

Look at the BARB TV viewing charts for the years 1998, 2002 and 2007. They give an impression of how television viewing has changed over the past ten years by channel.

It is important to know which television channels have the most viewers and how viewing habits change in order to ensure the popularity of a television channel and therefore its success as a business. BBC Television gets its funding from the television licence and the company must justify its use of the licence money or the government may reduce funding if a channel loses too many viewers to ensure its sustainability. If it is a commercial channel that becomes unpopular, the advertising revenue required to make the programmes may be reduced because advertisers might not want to advertise. Retailers who advertise on television want exposure to the widest audiences so will move their commercials away from channels that are unpopular. The most successful channels are likely to employ more production personnel to make more popular programmes.

Task 1

Audience data

In a small group, brainstorm the reasons why BBC1 has been losing viewers. Who do you think would be interested in this information?

Task 2

Audience awareness

On your own, make a list of the five television programmes that your parents might watch. Make a similar list of the five television programmes that you watch.

Now, as a class, make a list of the five commonest programmes in each group. Together decide if there is any overlap in preferences between the two audience groups. Why might there be an overlap in the programmes that you watch and those that your parents watch?

When a new television series is broadcast, or a new computer operating system is released, the company tries to maximise the number of consumers who will view or purchase it.

Task 3

Product reach

In a small group, list the ways in which a TV channel would try to target a wider audience. When doing this, consider where they would look for their audience and the type of audience they would target. Present your findings back to the whole class.

When Windows Vista was marketed it was presented in a number of different versions. In a small group, list the reasons why you think there was justification in releasing more than one version. When you have done this, report back to the whole class and compare your reasons.

Audiences, or consumers as they are often called, don't all watch the same television programmes, listen to the same radio stations, buy the same magazines, listen to the same music or play the same computer games. Audiences are divided by marketing companies into groups according to a range of characteristics including age, social class, where they live, whether male or female and so on.

Depending upon the purpose and the organisation, a population (or audience) will be divided into age groups like the examples in the chart overleaf.

Group	Age
1	0–10
2	11–15
3	16–18
4	19–25
5	26–40
6	41–55
7	56–70

Organising an audience by age is probably one of the easiest and clearest methods of division. Small children are not very interested in news programmes and newspapers. Teenagers are not very interested in classical music. People of state pension age are not very happy listening to loud rock music radio. These are generalisations and there will always be exceptions, but the idea is to group people according to general tastes. This way a media product can be made to appeal to the greatest number in a group, and the group can be identified and targeted accordingly.

Below is reproduced the socio-economic classes grouping according to the UK Registrar General 1911 Census. This system grouped people according to their social class and gave each group a letter.

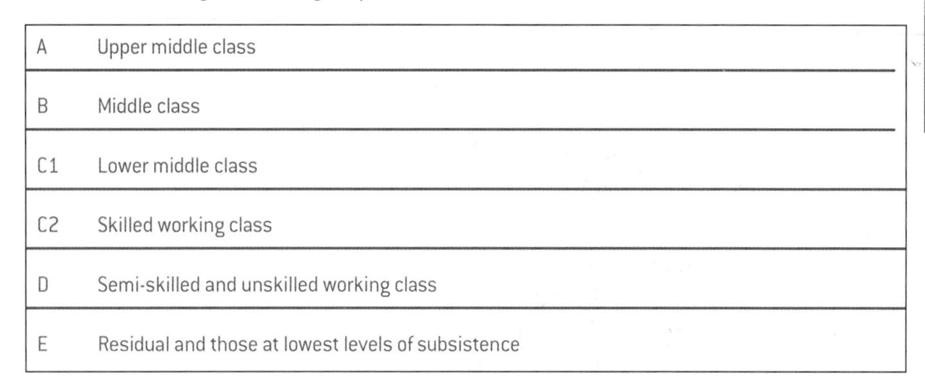

A	Upper middle class
B	Middle class
C1	Lower middle class
C2	Skilled working class
D	Semi-skilled and unskilled working class
E	Residual and those at lowest levels of subsistence

The chart below shows the Standard Occupational Classes or SOC devised by the Office for National Statistics & Economic and Social Research Council for use in the 2001 Census. This gives each occupational group a number from 1 to 9. You will find reference made to one or other of these charts when audiences are discussed.

1	Managers and senior officials
2	Professional occupations
3	Associate professional and technical occupations
4	Administrative and secretarial occupations
5	Skilled trades occupations
6	Personal service occupations
7	Sales and customer service occupations
8	Process, plant and machine operatives
9	Elementary occupations

It is worth noting that students are classed according to the group to which their parent with the highest income of the household belongs and that unemployed people are classed according to the last employment they held.

Write down four reasons why an understanding of socio-economic groups is useful for someone working in the media industry.

Task 4

Audience profiling

Working in small groups, scan through a listing magazine like the *Radio Times* or *TV Times*. Pick any weekday and identify which radio and TV programmes would be attractive to each age group. Now do the same with a weekend day. Note the change in the number of programmes for specific younger age groups.

Note the time that each programme is broadcast and that on television there is a definite watershed for programmes that depict violence, sexuality and profanity. On what day and times is the greatest concentration of children's programmes to be found? Can you explain why there is no watershed on radio?

Working individually, visit the website of a magazine publisher, eg IPC magazines or EMAP. See if you can classify the range of magazines by age group. Report your results back to the class. With magazines you will notice there is a more defined targeting between the sexes with obvious male and female magazines. Add the target gender of each magazine to your findings.

Now look at the socio-economic group charts and decide which group you fit into in each chart, remembering that your SOC is defined as being the same as that of your parents.

Using the same listing magazines, see if you can identify which programmes would be best suited to different socio-economic groups. You should use both charts as there is likely to be some overlap.

As a commissioning editor, would you use these tables? How would you use them? Would they be useful? Present your ideas back to the rest of the class.

Consumer behaviour

Consumer behaviour is constantly changing. Young people are spending less time watching television and playing outdoor games. There is also a greater uptake in downloading music from websites in preference to buying it on CDs. The consequence of these changes is that producers and manufacturers have to be constantly aware of how they can target their consumers.

Task 5

Conduct a survey of your class to find out how many hours per week are spent listening to radio, watching television, working on computers and reading papers and magazines.

Imagine you are an advertiser and you want to advise a client on how to target an audience in the 16–19 year age range. Write an email explaining which media would be the best option and why. Use your results from the survey to justify your recommendations.

With the help of your media tutor, devise a questionnaire and conduct a survey of the teachers in your school or college to find out their media preferences. Write a similar email to your client suggesting the best media to use to target tutors.

Consumer attitudes

What do you think about the television and radio programmes that your parents watch and listen to, and what do they think about your choices? Do you watch any programmes that your parents watch? Do you read the same types of magazines? Probably not! Different media products may have different content depending upon the target audience.

Task 6

Working in a small group, devise a questionnaire to establish people's views on the media that you are studying: television, radio, newspapers, magazines, websites, computer games. The purpose is to find out if the type of product you want to make has an audience, and if so, how it is defined. Media products are always made with specific consumer groups in mind.

TV Facts						
Annual % Shares of Viewing (Individuals) 1981–2006						
YEAR	CHANNEL					
	BBC1	BBC2	ITV 1 (inc GMTV)	C4	Five	Others
1981	39	12	49	-	-	-
1982	38	12	50	-	-	-
1983	37	11	48	4	-	-
1984	36	11	48	6	-	-
1985	36	11	46	7	-	-
1986	37	11	44	8	-	-
1987	38	12	42	8	-	-
1988	38	11	42	9	-	-
1989	39	11	42	9	-	-
1990	37	10	44	9	-	-
1991	34	10	42	10	-	4
1992	34	10	41	10	-	5
1993	33	10	40	11	-	6
1994	32	11	39	11	-	7
1995	32	11	37	11	-	9
1996	33.5	11.5	35.1	10.7	-	10.1
1997	30.8	11.6	32.9	10.6	2.3	11.8
1998	29.5	11.3	31.7	10.3	4.3	12.9
1999	28.4	10.8	31.2	10.3	5.4	14.0
2000	27.2	10.8	29.3	10.5	5.7	16.6
2001	26.9	11.1	26.7	10.0	5.8	19.6
2002	26.2	11.4	24.1	10.0	6.3	22.1
2003	25.6	11.0	23.7	9.6	6.5	23.6
2004	24.7	10.0	22.8	9.7	6.6	26.2
2005	23.3	9.4	21.5	9.7	6.4	29.6
2006	22.8	8.8	19.6	9.8	5.7	33.3

Task 7

Competitor analysis
Look at the BARB viewing figures charts for 1981 to 2006 for the different networks. There are significant trends in the way audiences have consumed the content of each network.

- What factors are responsible for these trends?
- What are the implications for the owners of these networks?

Imagine you are producing a television programme of your choice. Based on this information, decide which channel you would want to approach. Referring back to the listings magazine used earlier, see if your choice of programme type appears in the channel schedules.

Advertising placement
From the activities already completed it will be clear that different people watch television and listen to radio at different times of day, and days of the week. Radio and television are different from magazines, newspapers and websites because consumers choose them and consume them at times convenient to themselves. TV and radio is happening all the time and with the exception of the audio and video recorder, programmes are consumed at times that appear to be dictated by the media producers. However, we also know that certain programmes are broadcast at certain times and that these times coincide with when the specific groups of consumers are generally available to access them. The same applies to advertising, and adverts are broadcast when the target group is accessing relevant programmes. It follows then that advertisements targeting these audiences will be broadcast either during, before, or after the programmes.

Task 8

Working as a small group and making reference to back copies of listings in magazines like *Radio Times*, *TV Times* etc, decide which advertisers would want to air commercials on specific networks and which would be the best times to maximise revenue. Present your ideas, with reasons, to the rest of the class.

Advertising effects
Advertising has a number of knock-on effects – for example, peer pressure can cause everyone in a target group to want the same product. This could mean that some people will go into debt to get something, or that they will spend money set aside for essentials like food and bills in order not to be left behind.

Task 9

Think of a radio, TV or web advertisement that has caused you to buy something and answer the following questions.

What was it in the advertisement that was most persuasive? Was it image, peer pressure, lifestyle, fashion leader, feel-good factor, brand name, any other factor? List these factors in order.

On your own, collect a number of magazine advertisements. Then, working in a small group, produce a portfolio of advertisements grouped according to the persuasive technique used. How well do these persuasive techniques work? Analyse your portfolio and write up your findings.

ACTIVITY 2

PRODUCTION RESEARCH

There are two broad divisions for production research: resources, and programme content. The first consideration in production research for a media product is to establish the viability of successfully producing the product that you have in mind. You need to consider the timescale for the project and whether you are trying to be too ambitious and whether the content is going to be available.

Product content

In deciding on the content of a radio or television programme, newspaper, magazine, website or computer game, consideration must be given to whether there will be an audience for it. The target audience will dictate to a great extent the format, structure and style of product and the use and type of music. The format structure and style of a product should not be confused with the genre of the product – for example, television genres include soap, natural history, reality, western, crime etc, but can be given different treatments, structures and styles that will make them appeal to different audiences. Examples of different styles of quiz programme targeting different audiences would be *Have I Got News For You* and *Mastermind*. *Grange Hill* and *Coronation Street* are two soaps that are targeted at different audiences. *Newsbeat* on Radio 1 and Radio 4's *Six O'clock News* are two news programmes targeting different audiences. The content of a product doesn't dictate the style, format or structure, and media products are often hailed as new genres because they are the result of the application of a different style, format or structure to content that has been presented in the same way for a long time.

Task 1

In a small group with two or three classmates, select a topic for a media product. Referring back to your market research devise a different style, format and structure. Describe the scenes or elements, putting a structure to your idea along with each timing of individual element. It is important to plan in this way to ensure that the production is not simply a copy of other products.

Consider where you would find contributors, who they might be and how you would get them to agree to contribute.

Next, consider where you would find background information for the topic and how you would validate it.

Resources

You must consider the resources that are available to you to produce this programme. Your college or school should have video cameras, microphones, audio recorders, video edit workstations, computers with word processing, web authoring, page assembly and digital graphics software on them. However, there may not be sufficient for every member of the class to use the equipment at once and the production process dictates that equipment is only used when it is required, eg while planning the product, no acquisition equipment will be required. For a shoot or a recording, only a camera or audio recorder will be used; and for editing, the editing software will be needed on the workstation. In the media industries, resources must be booked and hired out from appropriate companies. To reduce costs the equipment is only hired for the period of time that it will be required.

Task 2

Working in your small group, produce a list of all the equipment that you will need to make a media product appropriate to your chosen media pathway. You should produce a production timeline showing where and when each piece of kit will be needed. This means knowing how long each stage of the production process is going to take. Share your list with the rest of the class.

Personnel
Production personnel must be engaged to make any media product. In this instance they will be members of your class. The sort and number of roles will vary according to the media pathway you are following.

Task 3

Bearing in mind the range of skills required, which includes researcher, interviewer/reporter, presenter (for radio and TV), writer, camera operator (for video), sound recordist (for audio), graphic artist (for website) and editor, list those members of your class who you would want to be in your team, the role they should perform and when, during the production timeline, they will be needed. The director/producer is your teacher/tutor. Share your list with the rest of the class.

'Talent' is the word used in film and television for the actors and presenters who will be seen on camera. This may include members of your class or you may have access to a drama group or other source for your talent. Others who participate in the production of media products are called contributors and may be experts in their particular field or have particular roles or status. Remember that contributors are not always used directly in a media product. A contributor may be interviewed for their expertise or simply to get an opinion. Their responses may be written as a script and the part re-enacted by another or, in the case of a text product, the words may be included in the article as direct speech.

Task 4

Make a list of all those who would contribute material to the content of your product, listing what specific material they would contribute. Explain how you would persuade them to contribute, eg personal kudos, vanity, sense of duty, etc. Produce a talent-release form that will be signed by each contributor. Share your list with the rest of the class.

Finance
You may not have any budget to work with but you must consider where you would get the necessary finance from if you were making a product professionally. Finance is used to pay for hire fees for equipment and personnel.

Task 5

List the sources of finance for media products according to your chosen pathway: BBC Radio and TV, ITV 1, Channel 4, independent commercial radio programmes, newspapers, magazines, websites, computer games.

Based on this and according to the media sector your are studying, make a list of where you might get the money to make your media product.

Suppliers
Consider the materials you would need in producing a media product appropriate to the pathway you are studying. This should include media like software licences, video tapes, audio discs, CD blanks for production of interactive CDs, DVDs for production of videos, vehicle hire, materials for sets, consumables like paper, ink for printers, catering, etc.

Task 6

List all the material you would need to purchase, with quantities and prices.

Decide which suppliers you would need to have accounts with if you were an independent professional producer, find and list their websites and addresses. Share your list with the rest of the class.

Facilities includes studio, rehearsal rooms, dubbing and editing suites, interview rooms, offices, photocopying, photo and film archives, etc.

Task 7

Make a list of all the facilities you are likely to need. Produce a copyright clearance form. Share your list with the rest of the class.

Locations are used when making television programmes and some radio programmes. When locations are used, permission must be sought from the owner (remember that everywhere is owned by someone). A full recce must be completed for each location and check sheets and risk assessments completed to comply with the Health and Safety at Work Act (1975) and subsequent legislation.

Task 8

List the locations you would need and from whom you would need to obtain permission. List all risk issues that must be addressed for each location you have identified. Create an appropriate permissions sheet for each location. Share your list with the rest of the class.

Logistical support

Logistics is the business of managing and controlling the progress of the production from start to finish, making sure that everything that is needed will be there when it is needed. It includes organising contributors, location shoots, transport, facilities, suppliers and finance, and ensuring that the programme comes in at the lowest possible cost. To do this requires the whole production process to be planned in advance using a production schedule.

Task 9

Using flip chart sheets and working in a small group, draw up a production schedule for your programme from start to finish and include everything you can think of. Display this on the classroom wall.

Costs

When you make a media product on your course you will have free access to a range of equipment and you will also have your class time to spend on the project because you and your classmates are on a course. However, in industry the equipment must often be hired specifically for making the product and even if you were a production company that owned its own kit, you would have to include in your estimate the cost of wear and tear on the equipment you are using and the cost of replacing it after a number of years. Either way there is a cost involved. Similarly with time, the number of hours you would spend if you were a professional programme maker would need to be charged, otherwise you would never earn a living!

Task 10

Working in a small group, compile a budget, as if you were a professional production company, to show how much it would cost to make a media product appropriate to the pathway you are studying. You can get current rates for equipment from hire companies and rates for TV, film and radio personnel from the BECTU website. Other rates can be obtained by visiting the appropriate websites for the sector being studied. Display your budget sheet on the wall.

Viability

Is your programme going to be viable? Two effective tools for establishing the viability of a programme are a SWOT analysis and a PEST analysis. SWOT is an acronym that stands for Strengths, Weaknesses, Opportunities and Threats.

The **Strengths** of any product should first include the content – otherwise the product will be destined to fail. Other strengths could be the valuable purpose of the idea, whether it is raising awareness about a topical issue, or educating, informing or simply entertaining people. Production strengths might include a relatively low budget, content that is easy to acquire, etc.

The **Weaknesses** of a product might be that it is not feasible to make, the concept is not quite right or perhaps the content is distasteful to certain audiences. The logistics of a project must be considered. Raising money may be difficult (funding is fundamental to any project in the real world) or it may not be easy to acquire the content.

The **Opportunities** opened up by a product might include such things as the chance to communicate to the masses, raising awareness, tackling important issues and educating people. A product on smoking, for example, could help reduce the number of people who smoke and therefore improve health. Such opportunities depend on the content of the individual product, but they can be a great asset.

The main **Threats** are the unknown problems that might (and probably will) crop up in the production and post-production stages. Their impact can be greatly reduced if the potential problems that can be anticipated are identified and assessed in the planning stage and, hopefully, eliminated. Other potential external threats can include competitors advertising the broadcast of similar programmes, publication of news stories, features and articles by rival print organisations and the restriction of production budgets through loss of advertising revenue. Many potential threats can be pre-empted by good planning to ensure that appropriate personnel and equipment are going to be available.

Task 11

Conduct a SWOT analysis of your programme listing the relevant Strengths, Weaknesses, Opportunities and Threats under each heading, addressing the following points:

Personal interest

Knowledge of subject

Accessibility to contributors

Availability of primary information

Availability of secondary information

Research skills

Time management

Contribution to CV/showreel

Human resources

Physical resources

Knowledge of equipment

Communication skills

Topicality, currency, relevance

Access to locations

Sensitivity of content

Authorisation

Copyright

Budget and costs

Disclosures/confidentiality

Exclusivity of discourse

Access to unconventional sources

Codes of practice

Sources of information

Time scale/availability

Need to adhere to ethical practices

A PEST analysis is a step further and considers the Political, Environmental, Social and Technical issues that may arise as a result of making your product.

Political implications may be present in any product that takes political sides and either supports or criticises, by its treatment of the content, any political group, either in power or opposition.

Environmental issues are often the subject of media products and far-reaching environmental effects can occur by publicising certain things; for example, some years ago there was a television series called *Food for Free*, which identified where people could pick edible wild mushrooms. The effect on the environment was devastating as droves of tourists swooped on the area to pick wild mushrooms and the area had to be sealed off.

The **Social** impact of the content of a media product on an audience, particularly if it is a large audience, can be significant. The government in the 1970s published a pamphlet about nuclear warfare called *Protect and Survive*, in which totally inadequate advice on how to survive nuclear war was offered to the population. The outcome was disastrous and pressure groups were enabled to highlight the shortcomings, causing a debate that lasted for a very long time.

Technical constraints may well affect the viability of a media product; for example, if the intention was to make a natural history programme halfway up a mountain or to publish a work on nanotechnology, the means to photograph the images would cause some technical problems: in terms of the size of the cameras needed either being too big to be hand-held on the end of a climbing rope; or not able to record the images required because the subject material is too small to photograph.

Task 12

Compile a PEST analysis on the media product that you intend to produce, listing the issues under each of the four headings.

Placement within the schedules

It is important that your media product is made available to its audience in an appropriate way. Once you have decided on the type of product, you must consider the way in which it is to be accessed by the target audience. For radio and TV programmes this means finding the correct slot in which to broadcast the programme. For a publication like a newspaper or magazine, the distribution is via newsagents and bookshops where the product must be displayed in the appropriate section. For websites, the key word used in a search engine is important to enable it to be searched. Computer games need to be packaged in the most attractive way for the target audience.

Task 13

For a TV or radio programme, by referring to schedules listed in magazines, identify a broadcast slot for your programme. In doing this you will need to have identified the target audience and decided on the channel they would watch, the time of day, and day of the week. You should also consider whether your target audience would choose to record the programme to be viewed at a time of its own choosing and the relevance of whether this was an option for the broadcast slot. For a newspaper or magazine, explain how the front page or cover could appeal to the target audience. If a website, state what key words describe your product best to its audience. For computer games, design a visual image for the box that illustrates your game.

BE ABLE TO APPLY A RANGE OF RESEARCH METHODS AND TECHNIQUES

This section focuses on grading criteria P2, M2 and D2 from Unit 1 – Research Techniques for the Media Industries.

In the previous activities you were introduced to the reasons behind the need for research when making a media product. The following activities will develop your understanding of research to an even greater degree and you will produce research for a specific programme that you are going to make as part of an integrated brief.

For the following activities you will be using a range of **resource procedures** that include search methods such as: subject indexes, search engines, book catalogues, book loans, reservations, borrowing materials, consulting reference-only sources and interlibrary loans service.

ACTIVITY 3

AUDIENCE RESEARCH

There are two main types of research: primary and secondary. Searching for information in appropriate records is secondary research, but doing a survey of your own in the street, asking people questions and writing down what they say, is primary research.

Each of these methods can be used to gather quantitative or qualitative data. The method used will be dictated by the data required. Quantitative data is statistical in nature and will be recorded as figures and numbers – the size of audience for a particular television channel, for example. To establish the audience's responses to a programme requires open questions and subjective verbal or written answers, thus producing qualitative data.

Secondary sources
Secondary research is useful for establishing the reaction to media products when they were broadcast or published. Reviews of films, TV and radio programmes are indicative of their success. Broadcasters often have an audience response programme like *Feedback* for BBC radio programmes, and the listing magazines have audience review columns. Magazines and newspapers usually have readers' letters columns where comments can be printed. Websites, while having their own user feedback options, can carry audience feedback for media products. Amazon has a review option on its website.

Task 1

Individually, gather **secondary quantitative** data on audiences for an existing media product of your choice. Search sources that will provide statistical data, eg BARB, about the size of the audience. This data can be used to justify your choice of a similar programme type to a commissioning editor/client.

Task 2

Individually gather **secondary qualitative** data on audiences for an existing media product of your choice. Search sources that will provide data to support the style content and format of a similar programme, eg the website of the targeted TV channel, programme reviews, etc. This data can be used to justify the content of your programme to a commissioning editor/client. Prepare a short verbal presentation for the client.

Primary sources

Primary sources are those from which you organise the collection of data yourself. It usually means organising a survey, preparing a questionnaire and conducting the survey to find out first-hand what people think about the idea that you intend to propose.

Task 3

Gather **primary quantitative** data in the form of a survey of statistical data on the level of interest from your target audience for your programme. Utilise **consumer categorisation** by identifying your survey sample from the socio-economic group tables and consider carefully the types of question that you will ask and the sample that you will target in your survey. In constructing your questionnaire, consider how you will obtain yes/no answers that you can turn into statistics.

Task 4

Tally the responses and analyse your audience surveys, *interpreting results*, and make notes of your findings, drawing conclusions and making recommendations to be used in the presentation to justify your programme. Present this to the whole class.

Task 5

Gather **primary qualitative** data in the form of a second survey of the target audience, which justifies the content of your programme. Utilise **consumer categorisation** by identifying your survey sample from the socio-economic group tables above and consider carefully the types of question that you will ask and the sample that you will target in your survey. In constructing your questionnaire, consider how you will use open questions to obtain answers that will support your approach to the content of the programme. Display all the questionnaires on the classroom wall so you all have an opportunity to see what other groups have done.

Task 6

Tally the responses and analyse your audience surveys, *interpreting results*, and make notes of your findings, drawing conclusions and making recommendations to be used in the presentation to justify your programme.

ACTIVITY 4

PROGRAMME RESEARCH

The content of the programme should be researched to establish whether or not the topic has been covered previously and, if so, in what way. Using the work of other producers is a good way of learning what can be achieved in your own production work. It may be appealing to do something that is new but it is worth finding out whether it really is new or simply that you haven't seen it done before. One of the ways in which programme makers break established conventions is by applying different treatments to a particular topic or programme content. For this reason it is appropriate that other programme forms and styles of presentation are investigated. By changing the style of presentation a programme can be made to appeal to an entirely different target audience.

QUALITATIVE SECONDARY SOURCES

Task 1

Investigate work of similar content by watching four programmes that deal with the topic you have selected, making notes about programme structures, content and format that will work for your programme. Analyse the data that you collect, *interpreting results*, and make notes of your findings. This will form the basis of part of your report.

Task 2

Investigate work of different content but of a similar style and format to that which you anticipate using, making notes about programme structures, style and format that will work for your programme and appeal to your target audience. Analyse the data that you collect, *interpreting results*, and make notes of your findings. This will form the basis of part of your report.

Task 3

Find programme reviews in schedules and listings magazines or on websites that give opinions on the treatment applied by the producer. Analyse the data that you collect, *interpreting results*, and make notes of your findings. This will form the basis of part of your report.

QUANTITATIVE SECONDARY SOURCES

Task 4

Search programme archives to establish the number of programmes that have been broadcast similar to the one you intend to produce. Analyse the data that you collect, *interpreting results*, and make notes of your findings. This will form the basis of part of your report.

QUALITATIVE AND QUANTITATIVE PRIMARY SOURCES

Task 5

Investigate the motivations of four programme makers who make programmes similar to the one you have chosen, using interviews either face-to-face or by telephone or email contact. Lists of relevant individuals can be found in programme listings in *Radio Times* and in the independent producers' list on the BBC Radio 4 website. Analyse the data that you collect, *interpreting results*, and make notes of your findings. This could form the basis of part of a report.

BE ABLE TO PRESENT RESULTS OF RESEARCH

This section focuses on grading criteria P3, M3 and D3 from Unit 1 – Research Techniques for the Media Industries.

ACTIVITY 5

The findings of the research carried out in preparation for the production of a media product should be formed into a written 'Treatment', the contents of which will be presented or pitched to the client or commissioner as a 'Proposal'. This will be done with the aid of a PowerPoint presentation to persuade them further that the product ideas, style and content are going to work. A written treatment will also provide all the information necessary to allow a third party to produce a product.

Producing the treatment
A treatment for a radio or television programme will contain a series of headings like those below. Each heading will carry specific information. Look at the list of headings below and the information each should contain.

Production team: Names, contact details. Each team member will fulfil the role of: researcher, camera operator, interviewer and editor

Programme working title and why it was chosen

Topic: What the programme will be about

The main message of the programme: What the audience will learn

Conflict: Opposing point of view of contributors or topic

Resolution: How the programme will reconcile the conflicting issues

Audience: Description of typical target audience

Contributors: List of contributors and experience, knowledge and points of view they will bring to the programme

Elements or scenes: Description of each scene and its purpose in the programme

Interviews: List of all contributors, whether or not they appear in the programme

Programme structure: Description of the structure of the programme, referenced to programme research findings

Form and style: Description of the form and style of the programme, making reference to examples of programmes and target audiences researched

Task 1

As a small group, read each heading and what it should include. Select one main heading each (excluding the first two) and for a media product that the group has chosen, list everything that you would want to put under your heading. List all the information on a flipchart sheet and display it. Look at what other groups have put on their sheets and make a note of anything you might have missed.

Task 2

Pick another media product and repeat Task 1, changing the heading that you completed. Again, share your work first with the group and then with the class.

There are a number of ways to compile a bibliography of source material and you will have to use one or more of them in your work. The three in most common use in the UK are: Harvard, MLA and ASA.

Task 3

Working in a group of three, select from the following as many as apply to the pathway you are studying: a book quotation, a newspaper, a magazine article, a website, a film, a video, a radio programme. Select one different bibliographic style each and write citations for each of your selections in your chosen style. Check each other's citation against the correct way of writing and share your work with the whole class.

You will need to prepare and present PowerPoint slides many times in your course when you pitch for a commission. PowerPoint is an easy presentation system and by following the Wizard you can produce a number of professional-looking slides quickly and easily. You will start with a title slide and a master slide that dictates the style of your presentation. You can select from a wide range of styles and you can import different backgrounds to personalise your presentation.

For a pitch you will need a slide for each of the headings that you used in the treatment, because this is really another way of presenting and reinforcing the treatment.

Task 4

Working in a small group, and using the media product you chose in Activity 5, Task 1, write the content for three of the slides (except the title slide) and ensure that you include reference to all the content listed against each slide title you choose:

Programme title: name of programme and sub-title description

Production team: list of team members

Programme topic: subject matter

Message: what the audience will learn

Conflict: opposing views covered

Resolution: how the issues will be reconciled

Audience: define target audience

Contributors: all who are in the programme

Elements: schedule of scenes

Interviews: all interviews carried out

Structure: comparison with similar programme structures

Form and style: comparison with other forms and styles relating to audience

Conclusion: summing-up and final positive statement in support of programme

Task 5

When you are happy with what the slides contain, put the content into a PowerPoint presentation and print out handouts of six slides to one sheet of A4 paper. Cut them up and use them as crib sheets to pitch your treatment.

Task 6

Using the PowerPoint presentation and your crib sheets, practise presenting your three slides to the other two members of your small group until you can deliver it as a whole presentation. When you feel confident as a group, present the whole treatment to the rest of the class.

UNIT 2 – PRE-PRODUCTION TECHNIQUES FOR THE MEDIA INDUSTRIES

This unit focuses on grading criteria P1, M1, M2, D1 and D3.

Learning outcomes

1 Understand requirements for production
2 Be able to obtain resources for production
3 Be able to apply production logistics

Content

1) Understand requirements for production

Resources: eg funding sources, staff, talent, equipment suppliers, facility houses, outsourcing

Codes of practice and regulations: legal, eg copyright, health and safety; insurance, eg public liability, completion insurance; regulatory bodies, eg Ofcom, Press Complaints Commission (PCC), Advertising Standards Authority (ASA), Pan European Game Information (PEGI), Entertainment Software Rating Board (ESRB), British Board of Film Classification (BBFC); trade unions, eg Producers' Alliance for Cinema and Television (PACT), National Union of Journalists (NUJ), Broadcasting Entertainment, Cinematograph and Theatre Union (BECTU); trade associations, eg The Independent Games Developers' Association (TIGA), Entertainment and Leisure Software Publishers' Association (ELSPA), British Interactive Media Association (BIMA)

Background research: specialist advice; archives; libraries; internet

Archive research: clearances, eg Mechanical Copyright Protection Society (MCPS), model release, location release; libraries, eg photographic, film, video, sound, printed material

People research: eg contributor biographies, team or crew CVs

2) Be able to obtain resources for production

Equipment: eg vision (camcorders, stills cameras), sound (microphones, digital recorders, analogue recorders), lighting (studio, location, flashgun, tungsten), support equipment (tripod, boom, jib), hardware (computers, scanners, graphics tablets, printers), software (text editing, image manipulation, layout, design)

Personnel: eg photographer, camera operator, sound operator, production assistant, editor, reporter, graphic designer, artist, interactive media designer, sound engineer, quality assurance technician, 3D animator

Materials: eg archive materials, original materials, assets, audio, script, still images, animatics, graphics, interviews, costume, properties, recorded music

Gathering and collating: eg storing resources, logging resources, asset management

3) Be able to apply production logistics

Planning: schedule; budget; bookings; contingency

Budget: equipment, eg production, post-production; materials, eg tapes, compact flash cards, Minidiscs™, photographic paper; talent; team or crew; transport; hospitality; locations; clearances; contingency

Health and safety issues: health and safety legislation; risk assessments

Documentation: eg production schedules, call sheets, location plans, studio plans, logging sheets, scripts, shooting scripts, storyboards, mood boards, thumbnails

Planning logistics for production: eg team or crew, talent, management, production, support, equipment, materials, locations, location recces, studio, transport, catering, accommodation

Planning resources for post-production: eg facilities, hardware, software (image manipulation, sound mixing, graphics, effects), personnel (team or crew, editor, graphic designer, interactive designer, layout artist, sound editor, support staff)

Grading criteria

P1 demonstrate understanding of requirements for production

In order to achieve this criterion you will have to demonstrate that you have a clear idea of what is required for production. You will know about all the requirements for a successful production. You will be able to identify pre-production techniques, issues about regulation and how to conduct research. You may not be able to explain fully what these are and how they will impact on your own production work.

P2 apply gathering of resources for production with some assistance

You will be able to gather together the resources you have identified in your planning. You will need help from your teacher/tutor or from your colleagues to do this.

P3 apply production logistics with some assistance

You must use your planned materials, resources and equipment in the production process. You will do this with assistance from your teacher/tutor or colleagues.

M1 competently demonstrate understanding of requirements for production with reference to well-chosen examples

In order to achieve this criterion you will be able to talk clearly about pre-production, regulation and research techniques. You will illustrate your work with well-chosen examples that show you understand issues that will have an impact on your production work.

M2 apply gathering of resources for production competently with only occasional assistance

You will be able to gather together resources and be able to apply them to your production and post-production. You will make sure that everything you need is in place and materials have been obtained. You will have a range of pre-production documents that support your work. You will require limited assistance from your teacher/tutor or colleagues.

M3 apply production logistics competently with only occasional assistance

In order to achieve this criterion you will be able to put your plans into place. The work you have produced in planning will be demonstrated in the production process. You will require only limited assistance from your teacher/tutor or colleagues.

D1 thoroughly demonstrate understanding of requirements for production with supporting justification and elucidated examples

You will demonstrate that you have a comprehensive understanding of pre-production, regulation and research. You will be able to illustrate your work with examples that show you understand why and how you use pre-production techniques. Your explanations will be detailed and relevant to the pre-production process. You will be able to reference regulations and codes of practice to your own pre-production work.

D2 apply gathering of resources for production to near professional standards, working independently to professional expectations

You will have produced a wide range of pre-production documentation that supports your gathering of resources. Your work will reflect professional practice and this will be demonstrated in your documentation and in the way that you work with little or no assistance.

D3 apply production logistics to near professional standards, working independently to professional expectations

You will demonstrate that you can put your planning into practice and this will be obvious from a successful production. Your work will reflect professional practice, that is to say you will be working in a similar way to a professional in the media industries. You will require little or no support from your teacher/tutor or colleagues.

UNDERSTAND REQUIREMENTS FOR PRODUCTION

This section focuses on grading criteria P1, M1 and D1 from Unit 2 – Pre-production Techniques for the Media Industries.

ACTIVITY 1

REQUIREMENTS FOR PRODUCTION

It is essential that you understand what you will require for successful production. There are many things to consider when planning for media production. It does not matter what form the production will take as long as the planning is in place. Here is a typical brief from a client who requires the production of a short promotional video programme. You should read through it carefully.

Working Title: DrugwiseUK

DrugwiseUK is a national charity that provides information to young people about the danger in using drugs. They have a video programme that is in serious need of updating and they have approached you for help.

They have commissioned you to produce a short video that will be sent to a range of potential supporters of the charity. This video will provide these supporters with a clear picture of what the charity does and how they need support from national and local companies.

You have produced a proposal and pitched this to them. They have agreed to the proposal and now require you to plan the production. They have agreed that they will fund some initial development of your proposal. You have suggested that you will produce a treatment and then discuss this with them before production begins.

The video will need to be appropriate for an audience of national and local companies. The video will be distributed as part of their campaign due to commence in three months' time.

You need to understand the requirements for the production of this product. To do this you will need to undertake the following tasks:

Task 1

In order to start the pre-production process, you need to identify the resources you will need for production. Work with a small team and hold a brainstorming session. Note down all the resources you think you will need. You could produce a mind map or spider diagram to demonstrate what you have found.

Present the results of your brainstorming to the rest of the class. Ask them what they have found and note down any resources that you have not thought of.

You will now have to undertake an audit of resources to identify those you already have and those you will need to acquire. Work with your team to produce an equipment audit. You could use a template such as this to do the audit for your equipment needs or you could design your own form.

EQUIPMENT AUDIT SHEET

Equipment needed	**Available** **Y N**	**If not available, where to find it**
DV camera		
Tripod		
Microphone		
Lighting kit	available from the Drama Department	
DV tapes	4 available - can buy more from Currys	
Computer with editing facilities		
Editing software		
Premier Pro	only two machines have this software installed	

Task 2

You will also need to identify the personnel required for the production. You could use a form like this or devise your own.

Personnel required	Name	Contact details
Director	John Smith	09979 423197 john@bzproductions.net

Task 3

DrugwiseUK will be funding the video. However, you will need to agree costs with them. Draw up a budget form to identify all the pre-production costs. A suitable simple budget form is shown below.

Item	Cost
Researcher @ £100 per day for 3 days	£300

You may need to refer to trade journals such as *Broadcast* or visit www.bectu for information on pay and conditions. Use websites to find information about equipment hire rates.

Look back at Tasks 1 and 2 to see the resources you have identified and then complete your budget.

Task 4

You will need to be aware of the codes of practice and regulations for media production. This will involve:

Legal and insurance issues
Work with a partner to make a list of legal issues and a list of insurances you need to consider for your production. By the side of each item, indicate how you will ensure that issues are addressed and considered.

When you have completed your lists, show them to the rest of your class and ask them to compare your lists with the lists they have made. See if there are any things you have forgotten to put in your lists. Make a note of them.

Regulator bodies
Regulators' details can be found at their website addresses, for example: www.Ofcom.org.uk

Using the Internet, find out who the media regulators are. You could use a search engine to do this. Think about all the media industry sectors, not just sectors you may already know about such as television, film or radio.

Use a form like this to note the names and addresses of media regulators and the areas they cover.

Media Regulator	Areas they cover	Contact details

After you have completed this form, you must identify the regulations that you might have to consider when planning a programme such as the one for DrugwiseUK. Present this information to the rest of your class and explain why it is important to follow regulations.

Task 5

You will need to undertake background research for your planned production. You may need to use:

- Specialist advice
- Archives
- Libraries
- Internet.

When using these research facilities, you should keep clear records of what you have used and the source of the information.

You have been asked by your Principal to make a short video about your school/college. This will be shown at the next Open Evening. Work with a partner and undertake background research to make a short presentation to illustrate the proposed content of the video.

Task 6

You may also need to undertake some archive research. This might be to find old footage, photographs or music to use in your production.

Working with your partner, find the names and details of library sources of archive materials. You could use a form like this or you could design your own.

Name of archive	Material they hold	Contact details
British Pathé Limited	Film archives	www.britishpathe.com

You may also need to obtain clearances for using locations, people and music.

- Model release – a form that allows you to use someone's likeness in your programme.
- Location release – a form that grants you permission to use a location for a set time and cost.
- MCPS – the Mechanical Copyright Protection Society will grant rights to use copyright material for a production at a set cost.

What archive research would you need for your short video about your school/college?

Work with a partner to make a list of archive material and where this might be found. Think about old photographs of your school/college, staff and ex-students. Is there any film of the school/college or record of special events that have taken place?

Task 7

You will have to undertake research into the people you will need for your production. This may be the crew, talent (actors), interviewees, extras or contributors. You should ask these people to provide you with a CV so that you have a record of their previous work and contact details. You may also need a biography of any contributors you use.

Think about whom you would use to make the short video about your school/college.

With a partner, make a list of everyone you will need. Be sure to include all the crew, staff members, students and parents. Why not include the school/college governors and some local business people?

When you have made your list, show it to the rest of the class and ask them to show you what they have done.

Task 8

You have decided that the video could be longer and be presented to parents as they leave the Open Evening. Your Principal has no money to fund either the production or the making of copies. Can you think of any ways in which you could get some funding for this project?

Work with a partner to make a list of potential sources of funding. Think about local and national businesses or other organisations that might provide funds.

Show this list to the rest of your class and discuss with them their sources of funding. They may have thought of other potential sources. Keep a careful note of any sources that you had not identified.

BE ABLE TO OBTAIN RESOURCES FOR PRODUCTION

This section focuses on grading criteria P2, M2 and D2 from Unit 2 – Pre-production Techniques for the Media Industries.

ACTIVITY 2

In order to obtain resources for production, you should firstly produce a treatment. The treatment will outline all the requirements for production and provide the client with details of equipment, personnel and materials you will be using for your production. The treatment can go into further detail about the style and content of your programme. This will demonstrate to your client that you have gathered sufficient information for the production to go ahead.

Task 1

A treatment is the development of your original ideas that were prepared as a proposal. The treatment outlines the resources you will need, the materials you will use and the crew and actors you are going to employ. The treatment will contain sufficient information to allow a client to give the 'green light' to a production.

Work with a partner or a team to prepare a treatment. You could use the following template to create your own treatment or you could design your own form. Each of the headings should be used to provide information about the resources you have identified and will be using. The client should be given a copy of the treatment so that they can see what you intend to do and how much this will cost.

You could use the information you have gathered for the DrugwiseUK scenario or you could construct a treatment for another project of your choice.

A Treatment For A Video Programme

DrugwiseUk

Prepared By John Smith

Zero Productions

Date of preparation here

Client
DrugwiseUK

Copyright © year here

Treatment

Programme title:

Client:

Writer

Date:

Introduction

Style and content

Outline script

Storyboard/moodboard/thumbnails

Outline budget

Contingency

Talent

Production staff

Task 2

You will need to identify all the equipment you will need for the production of your product.

Working with a partner or a small team, produce an equipment checklist similar to the audit document you produced earlier. This checklist will be more detailed and you will be able to identify clearly what you need and where it can be found.

Equipment required	Available Yes No	If No, where can it be found
HD Camera		Can be hired from Gearhouse 01799 457988

Task 3

You will also need to identify the personnel required for the production. Work with a partner or a team to produce a personnel checklist like this. If you prefer, you could design your own checklist.

Personnel required	Available Yes No	Details
Camera operator		John Brown 07899 43251 johnbrown@yourproductions.com

Task 4

You will need to identify where the materials you will need for your production can be found. Work with your partner or team to complete a material form. To do this, you could use a form such as the one below, or you could design your own.

Material required	Located	Cost
Video tapes	Storage cupboard Only 3 left	More available at Big pockets.com @£5 each

Task 5

You will need to ensure that you have gathered and collated all this material successfully before the production process can start. You must work with a partner or a team to:

- Provide evidence of where your resources have been stored
- Provide copies of the checklists you have created.

These should be stored and used later in this unit.

BE ABLE TO APPLY PRODUCTION LOGISTICS

This section focuses on grading criteria P3, M3 and D3 from Unit 2 – Pre-production Techniques for the Media Industries.

ACTIVITY 3

This is the final stage of the pre-production process. This is the point at which you can demonstrate that you can apply the planning that you have put in place. To do this you will need to demonstrate:

- Planning – this will be copies of all your planning documents
- Budget – this will include all the costs for the production including contingency
- Health and safety issues – this will be your risk assessment documents
- Documentation – you will have copies of all the pre-production documentation you have produced
- Planning logistics – this will be the plans you have made to ensure that everything happens at the right time and in the right place for production and post-production
- Planning resources for post-production – this is the planning for resources you will need to edit the product.

Task 1

You will need to produce planning documents for your production. These will include a production schedule.

You should work with a partner or team to produce your own production schedule. This is a production schedule template that you could use or you could design your own.

Production Schedule Part 1

Programme title:
Client:
Writer:
Date:

	Date		Date
Programme started:		Completed:	
Proposal started:		Completed:	
Treatment started:		Completed:	
Agreement from Client:			
Shooting script started:		Completed:	
Storyboard started:		Completed:	
Production started:		Completed:	
Post-production started:		Completed:	
Rough-cut supplied to client:		Agreed with client:	
Final version completed:			

Task 2

Working with a partner or team, produce a final version of your budget. You have produced an outline budget in your treatment and now you will need a final version. You could use this budget template or design your own.

Production Schedule

Budget

Programme title:
Client:
Writer:
Producer:
Director:
Date:

	Cost	**Total**
Materials		
Equipment		
Actors		
Props/scenery		
Post-production		
		Budget £
Contingency 10%		Total Budget £

Task 3

You will need to undertake a risk assessment for your production. Undertake a risk assessment working with a partner or a team. You could copy this risk assessment form or design your own.

Risk Assessment Sheet

Programme title:
Client:
Writer:
Producer:
Director:
Date:

Major issues:

Solutions:

Contacts:

Emergency services:

Task 4

All your pre-production documentation should be stored in a pre-production file. This might be in written format or as a computer file.

Complete a document like the one on the next page, to make sure you have copies of all documents in your folder of work. You should put your name on each document and make sure you have indicated that it is your own work.

Pre-production documents	Yes	No	Where stored?
Proposal			File name – pre-prod/proposal

Task 5

You will have to ensure that you have all the resources for post-production available when the production phase has finished. Work with a partner or team to complete a post-production resources checklist. To do this you will need to complete a checklist such as this or design your own.

Resources	Details	Booked	Yes	No
Facilities:				
1 Edit suite	Room 47			
Hardware				
Software				
Personnel				
1 Graphic designer	Samina Khan			

Task 6

In order to demonstrate how you have undertaken the pre-production process, you should keep a pre-production diary. This will help you to remember what you have done.

Produce your own pre-production skills diary. Include all the activities you have done and record all the skills you have learned.

Here is an example of a pre-production skills diary. Use this or design your own.

Pre-Production Skills Diary

Activity undertaken	Date	Skills I have learned
I did a production equipment audit. I looked at all the equipment that I could use to make my product and made a list on an audit sheet.	13/04/2007	I have learned how to make an audit of equipment. This will help me to plan my production work. If I need other equipment I know where I can find it or if I have to hire or buy it.

This unit focuses on grading criteria P1, P2, P3, P4; M1, M2, M3, M4; D1, D2, D3 and D4.

Learning outcomes

1 Be able to originate and research ideas for a media product
2 Be able to pitch a proposal for a media product
3 Be able to manage the production process to create a media product

Content

1) Be able to originate and research ideas for a media product

Ideas: group and individual brainstorming; analysis of each idea; selection; justification

Audience research: age; gender; socio-economic grouping; lifestyle; location; audience figures, eg RAJAR, BARB, ABC, CAA, ELSPA, ChartTrack, MCV

Content research: primary, eg interviews, questionnaires, own observations; secondary, eg newspapers, magazines, books, audio, audio-visual, electronic, internet, archives, libraries; research into competitors, research into market

Constraints: time; costs; personnel; resources; legal and ethical considerations, eg privacy, libel law, defamation, race discrimination law, data protection, freedom of information; codes of practice; copyright (requirement, owner, clearance, cost)

Contingency: resources backup; logistics backup; time frame for project maturity

2) Be able to pitch a proposal for a media product

Proposal: content outline; target audience; resources; personnel requirements, eg cast and crew, team, specialists; budget; project schedule

Pitch: style; format, eg PowerPoint, video presentation, multiple presentation; technology, eg video screen, projector, audio playback; product information (content outline, target audience, resources, cast and crew requirements, budget, project schedule, market fit); preparation of materials; rehearsal of pitch; delivery of pitch

3) Be able to manage the production process to create a media product

Planning: agreed production roles; job allocation; task definitions and deadlines; agreed content outline within proposal; preliminary and regular team meetings; agendas and minutes; proposed schedules; logistics, eg personnel, equipment, locations, additional facilities, additional resources, risk assessment

Production management: pre-production phase; production phase; post-production phase; project management techniques, eg spreadsheet, dedicated software, agile methods, scrums; team and individual performance; contingency plans for staffing and resources; monitoring and reviewing; problem solving; prioritisation; crisis management; quality control; meeting submission dates; modifications after completion

Product: technical and aesthetic qualities; realisation of proposal; fitness for purpose, eg audience, client

Grading criteria

P1 originate and research ideas for a media product working within appropriate conventions

You will have thought of some ideas for a media product. You will have undertaken some research into the feasibility of these ideas. These will be obvious ideas that are capable of being made into a media product.

P2 pitch a proposal for a media product expressing ideas with sufficient clarity to communicate them and with some appropriate use of subject terminology

You will be able to pitch your idea to an audience or client. Your pitch will be sufficiently clear to enable the audience to understand your proposed idea. You will use some appropriate subject terminology in your pitch.

P3 carry out a management role in the production of a media product with some assistance

You will have to take a management role and demonstrate that you have fulfilled this role. You will have been supported in this role by a teacher/tutor or colleagues.

P4 create a media product working within appropriate conventions and with some assistance

You will have created a product that has not fully developed your potential. You will have worked to the best of your ability but may have encountered problems that you could not resolve. The product you produce will use appropriate conventions and have some shape and purpose. However, you may not have been able to produce it with flair or imagination. You will have received support from your teacher/tutor or colleagues.

M1 originate and research ideas for a media product competently showing some imagination

The ideas you produce and the research you undertake will show some imagination. You will move from obvious ideas to ideas that are practicable and well thought out.

Your research will help to develop ideas into workable products.

M2 pitch a proposal for a media product effectively expressing ideas with clarity and with generally appropriate use of subject terminology

In order to satisfy this criterion you will pitch your proposal using appropriate language and will do it with confidence. Your pitch will inform the audience about your ideas and will give them sufficient information to enable them to make a judgement about its suitability. You will have used appropriate subject terminology in your pitch. You will be able to respond to some questions.

M3 carry out a management role in the production of a media product competently with only occasional assistance

You will have managed a role showing effective and competent organisational skills. You will be able to communicate with your team and provide support for your team members.

M4 create a media product to a good technical standard showing some imagination and with only occasional assistance

You will have designed your product with some creativity and have started to move away from conventional techniques. The product will be competent and effective and you will have used imagination to produce the finished product. You will have required only occasional assistance from your tutor or colleagues.

D1 originate and research ideas for a media product to a quality that reflects near-professional standards showing creativity and flair

Your ideas, development and research will reflect professional practice. You will demonstrate that you can take ideas, undertake effective research and use the research to refine ideas.

D2 pitch a proposal for a media product to a near-professional standard expressing ideas fluently and using subject terminology correctly

Your pitch will be delivered with clarity and enthusiasm. You will use fluent language and presentation techniques to persuade your audience of the suitability of your proposed idea. You will use correct subject terminology and be able to respond to questions, giving accurate and concise answers.

D3 carry out a management role in the production of a media product to near-professional standards working independently to professional expectations

You will carry out your role showing a real commitment and using high-level organisational skills. You will be able to make decisions and be able to direct a team.

D4 create a media product to near-professional standards showing creativity and flair and working independently to professional expectations

Your product will be created using techniques and creativity that reflect professional standards. You will show high-level skills in using techniques and technology to produce your product. You will have shown that you can work without constant support and supervision.

BE ABLE TO ORIGINATE AND RESEARCH IDEAS FOR A MEDIA PRODUCT

In this section we will focus on grading criteria P1, M1 and D1 from Unit 3 – Production Management Project. Each of the activities will help you become more familiar with part of the content of the learning outcome.

ACTIVITY 1

THE BRIEF

HealthyEating.com is a national charity that encourages young people to eat healthy foods. They have been given a budget by the government to promote healthy eating using a number of activities. They have commissioned you to produce a short (five minute) promotional video that will be shown in cinemas across the country. The video will need to be appropriate for an audience of young people and the target audience will be in the 12–16 age group. The video will be shown in cinemas before appropriately certificated films.

The charity wants the video to be relevant to the target audience and you will need to consider how this might be achieved.

Task 1

Research into promotional videos

- On your own, make notes on what you think makes a promotional video successful or not.
- In class, brainstorm programmes that have been made to promote products or services. As a group, decide if these programmes have been successful or not.
- Look at as many of these programmes as possible. See how they have been made for a particular audience. Identify and note the techniques that the producers have used to promote the product or service to a particular audience.

Task 2

Think of an idea

As a small group, you need to think about an idea that you could use for the promotional programme for your client. Consider the programmes you looked at in Task 1. What could you do?

You will have to consider what you need to include in your programme. You may have to think of lots of ideas and then decide which one will work best. When thinking of ideas, take into consideration:

- The target audience
- The format of the finished product
- The length of the finished product
- The way that the product will be used.

You should present the results of your research to the rest of your class. You could do this using a presentation format such as PowerPoint. If you use a presentation you must produce presenter's notes to help you with the presentation. You should also produce a handout for the audience.

Task 3

In this case the product will be a promotional video aimed at young people in the

12–16 age range and it will be shown in cinemas. You should consider a number of ideas and then refine these until you come up with an idea that will work. One way to do this is by undertaking a mind map.

A mind map uses the principle of taking the theme or idea and thinking of as many ideas as you can that might work.

In your small group, try a mind-mapping exercise using the template below. You might want to copy it onto a flipchart sheet.

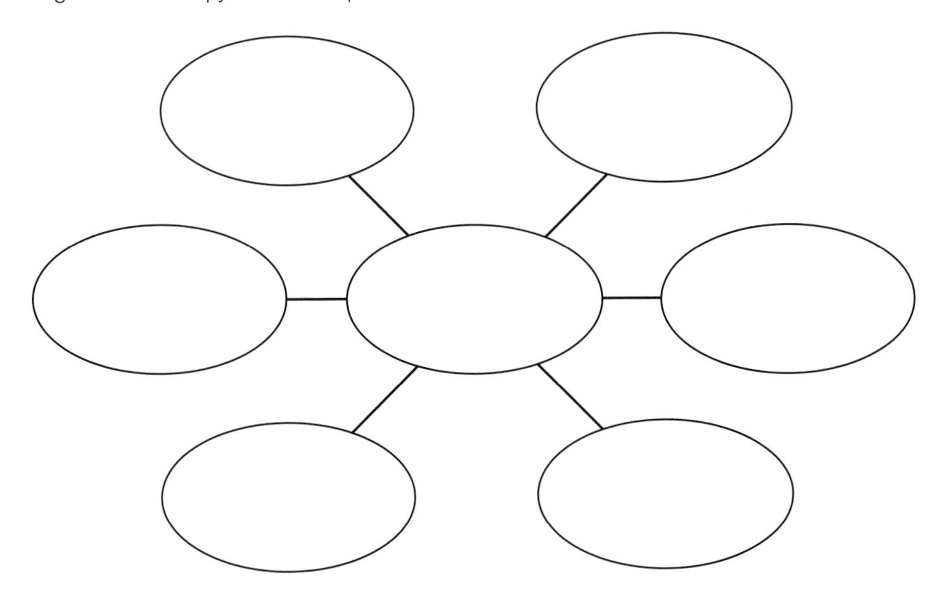

Task 4

Refining your idea

Once you have completed the mind map, you now need to refine your ideas. To do this you need to consider each idea in turn. Ask yourself these questions:

- Is the idea appropriate for the target audience?
- Will I have the resources and time to make it?
- Do I have the expertise to make the product?

With a partner, start to refine your ideas. Go through all your ideas and start to discard ideas that may not work. You must come up with one final idea that you think will work.

Task 5

Audience research

You now have an idea and you need to consider how to ensure that the product can be made to address the target audience. To do this you will need to undertake research into the target audience.

With a partner, look at a range of products that are aimed at this audience. This might be advertisements, television programmes, computer games and magazines. Ask yourself:

- What is the style (colours, fonts, etc) of these products?
- What music has been used to attract this audience?
- What effects have been used?

You should look at a range of audience research figures to see what type of products might be attractive to this audience. You should look at:

- BARB – The Broadcasters' Audience Research Board
- RAJAR – Radio Audience Joint Research Limited
- ABC – Audit Bureau of Circulations Ltd.

Together, produce a wall chart with examples of the products you looked at.

Annotate the wall chart with your thoughts on these products and the potential audience for each one. Put this chart on the wall and ask the rest of your class to comment on it. Look at what they have produced and see if there is anything that you could have added to your chart.

Task 6

Content research

You will have to research into the style and content of your programme. You will have seen from your audience research what your intended audience like to see in a product.

To undertake your own research you should use your initial idea and ask a sample of your target audience for their thoughts on your idea. You could produce a sample of your idea or simply ask the audience whether or not they think your idea will be appropriate. You can do this in a number of ways:

- Produce a questionnaire – this should be written in such a way as to produce qualitative data on your idea
- Interview a number of the target audience
- Hold a focus group of the target audience – ask them to discuss your idea and measure their responses.

You will be able to undertake further research into your idea by looking at the content of professionally produced products using a library or the Internet.

Working with a partner, prepare a questionnaire. Use this questionnaire to ask a range of people their views on a topic.

You could use one of the topics suggested below or, if you prefer, a topic of your own choice.

- Is there any demand for a college/school weekly paper?
- The preferred end-of-year entertainment for your college/school
- What is your favourite film or television programme and why?
- Who is your favourite band or singer and why?

You could use a simple questionnaire like the one opposite.

Once you have the questionnaires completed, analyse the answers and find a way of showing the results of your questionnaire. This could be in graphical form, such as a pie chart. You could produce your results as a report that identifies how many people answered a particular question and what answers they gave. You could then present the results of your analysis to the rest of your class. This will help you to understand how to measure audience reaction to the content of your proposed media product.

Task 7

Constraints

You will have to consider the constraints that might affect the idea that you have thought of. These may include:

- Time – will I have enough time to plan and produce this video?
- Cost – will I be able to produce it within a budget?
- Personnel – will I be able to find people to help me to make it?
- Legal and ethical issues – will I be able to make the product without breaking any laws or infringing someone's copyright?

Working with a partner, make a list of all the constraints that will affect your product. No doubt, this will include the ones above. By the side of each constraint, note down how it might affect your work on a project. Feed back your findings to your class.

You may find that other people have found constraints that you had not considered. If so, make a note of these and consider them when you make your own products.

Questionnaire for HealthyEating.com

Your name......................................

Your age..........................

	YES	NO
Do you know anything about eating healthily?	☐	☐
Do you think it is good to eat healthy food?	☐	☐
Would you like to see more information about what healthy food is?	☐	☐
If this information was in the form of a promotional video would you watch it if:		
...it starred a famous celebrity?	☐	☐
...there was an upbeat music track?	☐	☐
...the video was five minutes long?	☐	☐
...the video was ten minutes long?	☐	☐

(and any more relevant questions you can think of...)

Task 8

Contingency

You will need to have a backup plan in place in case things do not go according to plan. If your initial idea is not going to work you will have to have another idea in the background. If the equipment you are going to use is no longer available, you will need to have made a backup plan to use as an alternative. It may be that your actor is no longer available, therefore you will have to have someone else in mind.

You should always allow for some slippage in the timescale for your production.

Work with a partner to identify the things you should put in a contingency plan. What would you need to consider and how would you be able to plan for an unforeseen event?

BE ABLE TO PITCH A PROPOSAL FOR A MEDIA PRODUCT

ACTIVITY 2

Once you have your idea in place and you are sure that it meets the needs of the audience, you should pitch this idea to the client. The pitch is a way of demonstrating your idea to the client. The client might be someone such as the Chief Officer of HealthyEating.com or it could be your teacher/tutor.

Task 1

Preparing a proposal

The proposal is a document that 'sells' your idea to the client. The proposal should clearly outline your idea and give the client a real idea of what you are proposing to produce. You could use the template below to write your proposal or design your own.

Work with a partner and prepare a proposal for the programme for HealthyEating.com or for another project of your choice. You could consider:

- A video or audio programme to promote your school or college
- An advertisement for a new confectionary product that only uses Fair Trade ingredients.

Make the proposal as exciting as you can. Remember the proposal should sell your idea to the client or audience.

A Proposal For A Video Programme

Title here

Prepared by *Your name here*

Your company name here

the date here

Client name here

Copyright © year here

PROPOSAL

Prepared by
Your name here

Outline of idea

The style of the product

The content of the product

The way it meets the needs of the client and audience

Who will work on the product

The estimated cost

When it will be ready

Why this idea will work

End

You must remember to use correct subject terminology when writing your proposal. It is essential that media professionals use the correct language when preparing their documents, as this shows a client that they are media professionals.

Task 2

The pitch

You should pitch your proposal to the client using an appropriate method. This could be:

- A presentation using appropriate software such as PowerPoint
- A verbal presentation
- A video presentation
- An audio presentation.

Whichever presentation method you choose, you must ensure that you present your information in a way that demonstrates that you have thought about your proposal.

Work with your partner to prepare a pitch for the proposal you developed. The pitch should be illustrated with examples of how your proposal will work. You may want to include images or examples of your idea in the pitch.

For your pitch you should:

- Take equal parts in the presentation of your pitch
- Present your proposal, keeping eye contact with the audience
- Speak clearly
- Prepare presenter's notes to help with your pitch
- Use a range of expression in your voice
- Produce a handout for the audience
- Speak to the presentation slides or other material rather than simply reading it
- Include the audience by posing questions
- Be ready to answer questions at the end.

Remember to practise your pitch before you have to do it for real.

BE ABLE TO MANAGE THE PRODUCTION PROCESS TO CREATE A MEDIA PRODUCT

ACTIVITY 3

You have pitched your proposal successfully and you can now commence the production phase. To do this you will have to demonstrate your production management skills.

Task 1

Planning

You must undertake an initial production meeting to discuss the roles that need to be undertaken in the production process. It is likely that you will need to have a range of people working on the production of your product. You may be the person responsible for the whole production process or you may be responsible for one part of the process.

Work with a team and hold a production meeting and keep minutes of this meeting. In this meeting you should make decisions about roles. You could use the HealthyEating.com project or you could choose to work on another project.

In this meeting, record:

- The date, time and place of the meeting
- Who was present
- Who is taking the minutes
- What was said at the meeting

- Who is allocated roles in the production process
- Dates for stages of the production to take place
- The date of the next production meeting.

These production meetings must be held on regular basis. The minutes of these meetings will help you to monitor the progress of the production.

Task 2

Production schedule

You must produce a production schedule that shows when tasks will begin and when they will be completed.

Work with a partner to produce a production schedule. This could be for the HealthyEating,com project or another project of your choice. You could use a form such as this or you could design your own form. Keep this schedule in a safe place as it is a vital document in the production management process.

Production Schedule Part 1

Programme title:

Client:

Writer:

Date:

	Date		Date
Programme started:		Completed:	
Proposal started:		Completed:	
Treatment started:		Completed:	
Agreement from Client:			
Shooting script started:		Completed:	
Storyboard started:		Completed:	
Production started:		Completed:	
Post-production started:		Completed:	
Rough-cut supplied to client:		Agreed with client:	
Final version completed:			

Task 3

Logistics

You will have to manage logistics – whether for the whole production or for the section of the production you are managing. These might include:

- Personnel
- Equipment
- Locations
- Additional facilities and resources
- Risk assessment.

To do this you must keep comprehensive records to ensure that equipment, personnel and facilities are in the right place and at the right time.

Work with your partner to produce this second part of the production schedule. You could use this template to help you to manage logistics or you could design your own form.

Production Schedule Part 2

Programme title:
Client:
Writer:
Date:

Production equipment required:

Crewing requirements:

Actors:

Transport requirements:

Props/scenery:

Post-production requirements (format, effects, music, voice-over):

Task 4

Risk assessment
You must always consider the safety of your production crew and talent. In order to do this you must undertake a risk assessment. This will help you identify where problems might occur and what you can do to minimise the risk.

Work with your team or partner to undertake a risk assessment. This could be for the HealthyEating.com project or another project of your choice. You and your partner must consider all the problems you might encounter when undertaking the production of a project.

You could use a template such as this for your risk assessment, or you could design your own form.

Risk Assessment Sheet

Programme title:
Client:
Writer:
Producer:
Director:
Date:

Major Issues:

Solutions:

Contacts:

Emergency Services:

When you have completed your risk assessment, show it to the rest of your class and ask to see what they have done. By comparing work you may be able to find issues you had not considered.

Task 5

Production management
In order to manage the production process you will need to monitor the progress of production and post-production. To do this you should use a production diary that demonstrates how you have managed the process.

Working on your own, prepare your own production diary. Think about the way in which you will record this information. Should you do a written diary, a blog, a video or audio diary or some other method?

Your production diary should have dates and times of:

- Monitoring progress
- Where changes have been made
- Problems that have been identified and solved
- Modifications that have been made as a result of the monitoring process.

You must update your production diary on a regular basis.

Task 6

Product

You will need to undertake this task working as a team or with a partner.

Undertake research into the effectiveness of your finished product. To do this you should work together to decide how you will obtain feedback. You could show the work to a sample of the target audience. You could use the HealthyEating.com project or you could use another product you have produced.

Think about how you can obtain feedback. Do you:

- Produce a questionnaire?
- Interview people?
- Hold a focus group?

Whichever method you choose, you should make sure that you ask questions that are relevant and succinct.

The product should be measured against the following criteria:

- Its technical qualities
- Its aesthetic qualities
- Does it fulfil the initial proposed idea?
- Does it meet the client's needs?
- Does it meets the target audience needs?

Once you have obtained your feedback you should gather this together and analyse it. You should then present the findings from your feedback to the rest of your class.

In the media industries it is vital to obtain feedback from a client or an audience. The major film studios always show their latest releases to a sample audience for their feedback. If this feedback is negative the film is reviewed and, in some instances, re-shot or re-edited.

Think about your finished product and the results of your research.

- What could you change, and why?
- How would you make the changes?

UNIT 4 – WORKING TO A BRIEF IN THE MEDIA INDUSTRIES

This unit focuses on grading criteria P1, P2, P3, P4; M1, M2, M3, M4; D1, D2, D3 and D4.

Learning outcomes

1 Understand the requirements of working to a brief
2 Be able to develop a planned response to a brief
3 Be able to apply a response to a brief
4 Be able to review work on completion of a brief

Content

1) Understand the requirements of working to a brief

Structure of briefs: contractual; negotiated; formal; informal; commission; tender; co-operative brief; competition

Reading a brief: recognise nature of and demand implicit in brief

Negotiating the brief: consultation with client; degree of discretion in interpreting brief; constraints (legal, ethical, regulatory); amendments to proposed final product; amendments to budget; amendments to conditions; fees

Opportunities: identify opportunities for self development; new skills; multiskilling; contributions to project brief

2) Be able to develop a planned response to a brief

Plan: prepare plan to meet requirements; health and safety issues; relevant legislation to be followed; team members involved; role of team members; organisational structure; purpose and working practices if work experience brief

Timescales: deadlines; availability; resources; feedback

Develop: brainstorm; mind-map; identify possible solutions; treatments; scripts; programme/design formats; to meet requirements of brief; research potential of solutions; evaluate against requirements and constraints; select best option; discuss with client; agree final response

3) Be able to apply a response to a brief

Apply: pre-production phase; production phase; post-production phase; monitor progress; review; revise

Relationship with client: liaison with client; dealing with difficulties or complaints; revisions to brief; revisions to plan

4) Be able to review work on completion of a brief

Format: eg presentation; written report; viva voce

Constraints experienced: legal; regulatory; financial

Management: time management; leadership skills; communications; meeting requirements; achieving agreed outcomes; working to agreed timescales; recommendations for future tasks

Feedback: feedback from peers; feedback from client; feedback from audience; feedback from supervisor; contribution to workplace goals; own suitability for industry

Grading criteria

P1 demonstrate understanding of the requirements of working to a brief

You need to be able to describe accurately the requirements of working to a brief.

P2 plan a response to a brief, working within appropriate conventions and with some assistance

To get a pass you need to be able to produce, with the help of your teacher/tutor, a list of ideas that will show, using the correct techniques, how you intend to make a product that has been specified in a brief.

P3 apply a response to a brief, working within appropriate conventions and with some assistance

This means that to pass you must follow the plan you made to respond to a brief and that you should do it in a manner appropriate to the sector that you are studying, although you will need help from your teacher/tutor.

P4 describe and comment on your own work to a brief expressing ideas with sufficient clarity to communicate them and with some appropriate use of subject terminology

This means that you should not simply state what you did in the first three learning outcomes but give some reasons for specific key actions. You should also present it clearly enough to be understood and use some of the media terminology to which you have been introduced.

M1 demonstrate competently understanding of the requirements of working to a brief with reference to well-chosen examples

You need to be able to provide an explanation of the organisation and extent of a brief. You need to show clear examples of what you did in the process and explain what impact you had on the work of others and on the brief itself.

M2 plan a competent response to a brief showing some imagination and with only occasional assistance

A merit requires that you show in detail how you will produce a product that you have thought of yourself, based on the specification of a brief, with only minimal help from your teacher/tutor.

M3 apply a response to a brief competently showing some imagination and with only occasional assistance

To get a merit you must follow the plan that you made and you must do it very well, being creative, and do so with a minimum of help from your teacher/tutor.

M4 explain own work to a brief with reference to well-chosen examples, expressing ideas with clarity and with generally appropriate use of subject terminology

The merit goes further and asks you to state not only what you did to fulfil Learning Outcomes 1, 2 and 3, but to go into greater detail with your choice of examples and to do so clearly using media language in most of your answer.

D1 demonstrate thoroughly understanding of the requirements of working to a brief with supporting justification and elucidated examples

You will provide a full explanation of the organisation and extent of the brief. You will show a detailed understanding of your role, duties and responsibilites, as well as a thorough consideration of all requirements. You will need to show you have excellent communication skills.

D2 plan a response to a brief to near-professional standards showing creativity and flair and working independently to professional expectations

The difference between merit and distinction is that you have worked on your own as though you were in the industry, to show how you will produce a product that could be considered as good as one that had been produced by a person who does it for a living.

D3 apply a response to a brief to near-professional standards showing creativity and flair and working independently to professional expectations

Achieving a distinction means doing the job of following a production plan as though you were an industry professional, without help from your tutor, and achieving a product that is similar in quality to what you find being produced in the sector of the media industry that you are studying.

D4 critically evaluate your own work to a brief with reference to professional practice, expressing ideas fluently and using subject terminology correctly

A distinction requires that you reflect on what you have done in a self-critical manner, justifying your courses of action and explaining your reasoning in detail. The way that you express yourself is expected to be extremely good and the language must contain the correct media terms.

UNDERSTAND THE REQUIREMENTS OF WORKING TO A BRIEF

In this section we will focus on grading Criteria P1, M1 and D1 from Unit 4 – Working to a Brief in the Media Industries.

ACTIVITY 1

STRUCTURE OF THE BRIEF

This first activity is to enable you to become familiar with what a client brief is. Examine the example brief, sentence by sentence. The client is asking for a specific product to respond to a specific audience in a particular way. What the client is asking for may not be possible without some changes. The client is not providing any detail. That is for the production team to work out for themselves. There are many types of brief, depending on the client and the media sector. They include contractual, negotiated, formal, informal, commission, tender, co-operative and competition.

Typical brief for a radio series

Working Title: The Tees Valley now

Brief: BBC North East is seeking to commission a series of short programmes examining issues relevant to the Tees Valley and raising awareness of the significant progress that has been made in revitalising the area industrially, culturally and socially over recent years. The series would highlight some of the many initiatives and developments that have taken place and are ongoing in the area.

The primary target audience would be long-term residents of mainly B, C1, C2 & D socio-economic groups and those in SEGs B, C1 & C2 who have made their home in the area in the past few years to secure employment in the professions and managerial and white-collar occupational areas, both male and female, predominantly in the 25 to 40 age range and of Caucasian origin.

The series would also be networked on national speech radio and would therefore also have to appeal to a wider audience not resident in the Tees Valley.

The programmes would fill a projected 15-minute slot in the schedules at 3.30 or 3.45 Monday to Friday to coincide with national speech radio scheduling policy.

Programme proposals no greater in length than one page of A4 should be sent to the commissioning editor (your teacher/tutor) by xxxxxx date.

Task 1

Working as a member of a small group, examine each sentence of the brief and decide what it will entail to fulfil. Decide which type of brief it is from the list (given in the specification above) and give reasons. Present your findings back to the class.

Task 2

Working in a small group, decide which of the following categories this brief falls into: contractual, negotiated, formal, informal, commission, tender, co-operative and competition. Give your reasons. Where might each type be found? (This will require you to do some secondary research.) Share your findings with the rest of the class.

ACTIVITY 2

READING A BRIEF

Clients who don't work in the media industries often make assumptions when specifying briefs for media products. This is done more through ignorance of the implications of a specific requirement rather than through any attempt to get something for nothing. It is important, therefore, that the content of a brief is understood. The way in which a brief is written doesn't always spell out simply what is required. It is therefore important to read a brief and re-read it to see if there are any hidden expectations and assumptions being made.

The purpose of the following tasks is to help you prepare your own aide-memoire or prompt-list of considerations when responding to a brief. Working individually or as a small group with your teacher/tutor, make the following four headings on the flip chart or marker board: Physical constraints, Legal issues, Ethical issues, Regulatory constraints. Using the example brief:

Selection criteria applied to pitches by programme commissioners

- Does the proposal fulfil the brief?
- Is the programme physically possible?
- Is the timescale realistic?
- Does the programme fall within budget?
- Does it target the defined audience segment?
- Does it contravene any Codes of Broadcasting Practice?
- Will it be entertaining, informative, educational?
- How does it compare with the competition in all the above criteria?

Task 1

Individually, list all the physical constraints that might be implicit in this client brief and explain how you would respond to each.

Task 2

Individually, list all the potential legal issues (that is, where the law must be adhered to) that would need to be considered in fulfilling the terms of the brief. To do this you will need an understanding of how media law, particularly copyright, affects the product you are being asked to make.

Task 3

Individually, list all the potential ethical issues that would need to be considered in fulfilling the terms of a brief.

Task 4

Individually, consult the relevant codes of practice imposed by the regulatory body for the sector in which you are working. (You may need to do some research in the library or on the Internet.) Now list all the constraints imposed by regulatory bodies that would need to be considered in fulfilling the terms of a brief.

Task 5

Now refer back to your brief and, working in small groups, make a list of all the amendments to tasks 1 to 4 that might need to be negotiated before you reach final agreement of a client brief. Share these with the rest of the class.

Task 6

Working as a whole class, with your teacher/tutor as the client, produce a list of the areas that you must discuss with the client when negotiating the brief to produce a product that will be successful, using acceptable industry working practices.

ACTIVITY 3

OPPORTUNITIES FOR SELF-DEVELOPMENT

In responding to a brief there are many ways in which it can enhance self-development. Existing skills bases can be extended across different and complementary media sectors. Skills learned in one sector, eg writing for newspapers, could be transferred to radio or television programme scripting. There are differences of opinion about the benefits of multi-skilling in different sectors of the media industry. Some job roles, eg merging broadcast and print journalism, could be welcomed in some working environments, eg Rupert Murdoch's News International, where cross-media ownership might enable a journalist to work in radio, television and on a newspaper.

Task 1

Individually, list the **opportunities** for self-development that might be available if you had a work placement brief, and share them with the whole class.

Task 2

Individually, list the opportunities for self-development that might be available if you had a real client brief for the sector you are studying. Share your list with members of your class.

BE ABLE TO DEVELOP A PLANNED RESPONSE TO A BRIEF

In this section we will focus on grading criteria P2, M2 and D2 from Unit 4 – Working to a Brief in the Media Industries.

ACTIVITY 4

You now need to develop a planned response to the brief you have been given. The first stage of this task is to develop ideas for the creative content of the product. This refers to the planning stage of the production process where the content research is carried out. Experience of how similar types of product to the one being developed are made is essential and it is often advantageous to model a new product on one that is similar. The use of SWOT analysis helps test the feasibility of the ideas.

Task 1

Working in a small group, start with a session to brainstorm ideas for the product from which you will produce a mind map, spidergram or other initial written responses. You should produce some options for products, probably each with its own problems. Make a list of the best ideas and share it with your class.

Task 2

As a small group, identify and list possible problems for each product idea by means of a SWOT analysis to determine the Strengths, Weaknesses, Opportunities and Threats associated with each product. Use a flipchart and share your ideas with the rest of the class.

SWOT analysis chart

Strength	Weaknesses	Opportunities	Threats

Issues to respond to in SWOT

Any of these can be strengths, weaknesses, opportunities or threats, depending on the degree to which they impede or support your idea for a product.

Personal interest	Topicality
Knowledge of subject	Currency relevance
Accessibility to contributors	Access to locations
Availability of primary information	Sensitivity of content authorisation
Availability of secondary information	Copyright budget & costs
Research skills	Disclosures/confidentiality
Time management	Exclusivity of discourse
Contribution to CV/showreel	Access to unconventional sources
Human resources	Codes of practice
Physical resources	Sources of information
Knowledge of equipment	Time scale/availability
Communication skills	Need to adhere to ethical practices

ACTIVITY 5

By applying the SWOT analysis, which identifies the constraints of each idea in fulfilling the brief, your group should have narrowed the choices down to two or three viable options that meet the requirements of the brief and in a form appropriate to the media sector in which you are working. You are now going to do a PEST analysis on your product. The PEST analysis identifies the external factors that might affect your product.

Political ramifications could be present if you are addressing a politically sensitive topic. Political pressures may affect the content of the product and dictate how particular views and opinions are represented.

Environmental effects might result from your product, eg if you were making a programme about recycling or global warming, that might affect the behaviour patterns of consumers. You might also want to consider the effect that making the programme has on the environment: does the film need to be shot thousands of miles from home or could something as valid be shot closer to home?

Social change of a positive nature might occur as a result of producing a programme on care of the elderly or teenage pregnancy.

A programme on rock climbing raises certain technical issues, as does a drama to be shot in a protected environment.

The PEST analysis is also a useful tool when doing a thorough feasibility evaluation.

PEST analysis chart

Political	Environmental	Social	Technical

Task 1

Working in your small group again, apply the PEST analysis to the shortlist to see how much further the choice will be reduced. Hopefully there will be one choice that remains, but if there is more than one it is simply a matter of selection, or offering each option for the client to decide. Why not let the rest of your class decide for you?

Task 2

Having decided on one product, it should be developed into a proposal appropriate to the media sector in which you are working. It should be sent to your client with an invitation to attend a presentation of the proposal to be either at the client's premises or in school/college.

This is an example of a proposal for media product.

TITLE: The Changing Face of the North East

A documentary record in photographs, original music, verse, song, actuality and narration portraying industrial, environmental and social changes of the Tees Valley over 30 years

SYNOPSIS:

Creative photographer Ben Crewe was born in York in 1960. Specialising in environmental, industrial and social subjects, his work has been exhibited in the UK, Germany and Denmark and in educational establishments throughout the North of England.

The documentary will describe Ben Crewe's photographic archive of the changing face of the North East over 30 years. Revealing more than just his technical mastery, the discussion will recount his engagement with places, people and the way in which they experience life's joys, apprehensions, contentment, solitude and communion, and at the same time reflect on Ben's archive of rural, coastal and industrial objects, frozen in one timeless moment of their often ancient history.

Northern composer, lyricist and poet Brian Mills will be engaged in the role of narrator/presenter and some of his musical work and experiences of working in the environments described will be incorporated into the soundtrack.

The collaborative partnership of these two artists over more than 30 years is already renowned throughout the UK, through the release of photographic publications, CDs, live music performances and audio/visual presentations.

A handheld camera will record Ben Crewe conversing informally on location with Brian about his enthusiasm for taking photographs and the socio-economic symbolism of his life's work in the North East. The myriad images of people and places will be discussed in terms of confronting us as casualties of economic and social change and will be of significant value to viewers interested in contextualising their position within their evolved North East environment. Indeed, many photographs will evoke the uncertainties and doubts of a constantly changing society, as depicted by the image of the scarecrow buckled by the effects of too many ill winds, with which the viewer will be invited to align.

SUGGESTED ELEMENTS:

- On location, Brian Mills introduces the viewer to Ben Crewe and his career over opening shots of his photographic portfolio and a short sequence of Ben Crewe's community slide presentation.
- Brian Mills in vision walking and conversing with Ben, providing a link between each location and photograph.
- Discussions with people on location who will converse about the changes over the last 30 years, and commenting on issues relating to industrial, economic and social changes.
- Photographs of the original location would be shown with Ben debating the symbolism and socio-economic value of the photograph followed by Ben re-photographing the scene with a modern digital camera. The photographs would dissolve from old to new to make the changes explicit.
- Brian Mills' narrative, songs and music, which in themselves provide an audio document of the changing industrial, environmental and social face of the North East, will accompany the production.
- A montage of photographs accompanied by the music of Brian Mills will encapsulate the documentary.

BUDGET: approx. £10, 000

Task 3

Working in a small group and using the proposal as a guide, produce a PowerPoint presentation (three slides each) of the main points of your proposal and pitch (present) it to the rest of your class. If you are successful you will obtain confirmation of commission.

Task 4

Let's assume you have confirmation to proceed with your idea. You now need to agree on roles within your production team and, working as a team, produce a detailed treatment (including storyboards/mood boards if appropriate) that would be presented to the client for approval. Present your treatment to the rest of the class, take note of any feedback and modify your treatment if you think it would benefit.

Typical example of a treatment

Treatment for radio programme on recycling
Production team:

Jenny Walmsley	07770 64595
Kirsty Hersey	07780 86742
Chris Webster	07870 96846
Zin Zue	07637 62108

Programme working title: Recycling Change. I thought the name was catchy and said what we are doing.

Topic: A documentary to look at the environmental, political and social changes in the attitudes to recycling in the Tiddlebrough area.

The main message of the programme: To raise the audience's understanding of how important it is to recycle if the world is going to survive.

Conflict: Four conflicting issues:

1. Government is not putting enough money or effort into encouraging recycling.
2. Some people think that their little bit is just a drop in the ocean so they won't bother as long as the rest of the world is ignoring it.
3. Some people use more energy and time recycling than they are saving.
4. Industry isn't doing what it could to help.

Resolution: We will try to convince the contributors who don't recycle, by using those that do, and give a message to the audience that it must recycle to survive.

Audience: (in response to audience identified in initial brief) Men and women, aged 25 to 40, in most types of job, but in social class groups B, C1, C2 and D, because they are more likely to be listeners to BBC Radio 4.

Contributors:
Helen Shaw, Executive member for environment on council (Jenny's contributor)
Bill Kerr, Recycling officer in local recycling site (Kirsty's contributor)
Graham Black, Director of local company that uses recycled materials (Chris's contributor)
Members of public: men and women for Vox-pop (all of us did this)

Elements or scenes:
Introduction: Intro and menu, Presenter (in studio) sets scene and tells audience about current recycling situation.
Scene 1 Vox-pop male and female in town to get people's reactions to question: Do you recycle? Most people say 'No'.
Scene 2 Office interview with Helen Shaw where she explains what the council are doing and what they plan to do to increase recycling – reference to Vox-pop and attitudes.
Scene 3 Location interview near recycling unit with Bill Kerr to get an idea of how effective recycling is and whether it's worth it for financial reasons as well as for environmental issues.
Scene 4 Presenter explains about different types of recycling that doesn't mean the stuff has to be processed: charity shops, second-hand shops, hand-me-downs, websites like Myskip and eBay.
Scene 5 Location interview with Graham Black beside production line, who explains how his company makes new products out of the processed fibres, glass, paper and rags that are collected.

Scene 6 Second Vox-pop male and female on streets in town with informed recyclers contributing.
Close Presenter (in studio) makes case for recycling and thanks contributors.

Interviews: List here the people you will be interviewing and state whether or not they will take part in the programme or simply be sources of primary research.

Programme structure: The programme will be a similar structure to BBC Radio 4 programme *File on 4* or *Sunday Best* series. It will be presenter-introduced and linked, but the interviews will have the questions taken out and the contributors will say the questions in their answers, making it sound like actuality. No narration except maybe in the scene setting.

Form and style: The programme will take the form of an investigatory documentary putting the council man in the hot seat, accusing his council of not doing enough to get recycling going. It will be formal and use proper English because it's meant to appeal to an audience of intelligent people who like the style of *Material World*. The programme will be informative and educational but not really entertaining.

Task 5

Still working in your small group, look at the list of elements or scenes and, picking one scene each, individually write a draft script for your scene. Share your scripts with your group.

Task 6

Working in your small group, if it is a video product, take somebody else's draft script and individually draw storyboards for it. Share the storyboards with your group.

Other documentation that will need to be prepared includes: shooting scripts, locations permissions, talent releases and copyright clearances for archive material and music.

Task 7

In a group of four, select one of these document types and individually find out as much about it as you can using secondary research methods. Share your findings with your group and decide what should be included in the documentation.

ACTIVITY 6

In preparing the plan to meet the requirements of the brief, you must consider: health and safety issues, relevant legislation, production team and role of team members, organisational structure, purpose and working practices if responding to a work experience brief.

Task 1

In a small group, discuss the health and safety implications for each working situation that you might find in a production. This will include shooting or recording locations, the editing space and precautions when handling electrical equipment. Present your ideas to the rest of the class. When the other groups make their presentations, make notes of any ideas you had not thought of.

You have already looked superficially at legal issues, so now you need to look at relevant legislation that is likely to be an issue in the production process for a product for your sector.

Task 2

In your small group, pick one of the following legal issues (making sure it is different from the area that you worked on in the previous task): copyright, health and safety, employment contracts, public liability. By researching in the library or on the Internet, find out how the law affects your particular legal issue. Prepare a flipchart presentation for the rest of the class.

Task 3

Working on your own, imagine you are assembling a production team for a product in the sector that you are studying. Make a list of the production roles you would need to fill in order to make the product, and at what stage in the process they would be needed.

ACTIVITY 7

The timescales that apply to the production process are critical and must be planned accurately to enable the production to run to schedule. The production schedule is a timeline of the period of the production process from the moment the proposal has been accepted to the delivery of the product in an appropriate form acceptable for distribution to the audience. This means that timings have to be predicted for each task and each operation of the process and a contingency should be built in to allow for unforeseen problems.

Task 1

Individually, make a detailed production schedule to cover the whole of the production process including the planning, pre-production, production, post-production, audience testing and completion stages of the process that shows the timescales you have allowed for each task in the process. It will be necessary to check back to the SWOT and PEST analyses to anticipate every possible thing that could go wrong and to build in a contingency for such occurrences. Share your schedule with your small group.

BE ABLE TO APPLY A RESPONSE TO A BRIEF

In this section we will focus on grading criteria P3, M3 and D3 from Unit 4 – Research Techniques for the Media Industries.

ACTIVITY 8

Let us imagine you have successfully negotiated a brief with a client and you have been commissioned to produce a product. The planning is in place and you must now apply a response to the brief.

This means essentially keeping track of progress throughout the pre-production, production and post-production stage of the process. It includes the preparations that are made before acquisition (shooting, recording, writing or drawing the product content), the smooth running of the acquisition stage (filming, recording or gathering) and the progress of the editing. There are a variety of ways that this can be done but it is a matter of progress-chasing and taking appropriate action if problems occur and noting changes made to the original production schedule.

Task 1

Working as a small group, think of ways in which you could regularly track the progress of the production of a media product. Include in your list all of the tasks that you would need to complete, the people you would have to work with and those who you would have to inform in order to track production progress. Share your list and information with the rest of the class.

Task 2

Working in your small group, make a further list of changes and revisions that may have to be made to a production stage, the sort of problems that might arise to cause a change in schedule and the relevant individuals who might have to be kept informed of any such changes. Share this list with the rest of your class.

Task 3

Working in your small group, make a further list of changes and revisions that may have to be made to a post-production stage, the sort of problems that might arise to cause a review in schedule and the relevant individuals who might have to be kept informed of any such changes. Share this list with the rest of your class.

BE ABLE TO REVIEW WORK ON COMPLETION OF A BRIEF

In this section we will focus on grading criteria P4, M4 and D4 from Unit 4 – Working to a Brief in the Media Industries.

ACTIVITY 9

The completion of the product and its delivery to the client represents the fulfilment of the brief. To complete the unit you should review your work on completion of a brief. The choice of format for this task is optional. It could be a presentation, a written report or a viva voce (spoken one-to-one with your teacher/tutor) but must be agreed with your teacher/tutor in advance. The topics that you must cover, however, will be the same. The importance of being able to review one's own work objectively can't be over-emphasised. Critical analysis is essential in higher education and it is as well to learn the skill now. The practical outcome of the ability to reflect critically on the fitness for purpose of media products and the production process is better products that respond totally to the audiences for which they were created.

Task 1

Working as a small group, consider the activities that you completed on legal, regulatory and financial issues. Write down the constraints experienced by you individually in finding the information. Being objective, list the reasons why you had difficulty or why you found it easy to obtain the information.

Look back at the legal, regulatory and financial constraints experienced by you and the production team. Prepare a critical response drawing comparisons between your performance and professional expectations, that fully covers these three issues and justify the manner in which you responded to them.

Task 2

Working individually, consider the activities that you completed on the production management role and answer the following questions as fully and objectively as you can.

- How well did you manage your time while doing them?
- When working in your small group, how did you contribute to leadership of the group?
- How well did you communicate with your group members?
- How good were you at meeting the requirements, achieving agreed outcomes, working to agreed timescales and making recommendations for future tasks?
- What went well, and why?
- What went not-so-well, and why?
- How could you ensure better outcomes in the future?

Share your answers with your small group.

ACTIVITY 10

How well do others think you functioned when you were doing the activities? This is measured by the feedback that you obtain from peers (those with whom you were working, and classmates), your teacher/tutor, the audience for which the product was made (what did a sample target audience think of it?) and your supervisor (if this was a work placement). If this was a work placement, what was your contribution to workplace goals? In order to complete this part of the work, you will need to conduct some primary research to find their responses.

Task 1

On your own, ask the individual members of your small group how well they thought you contributed to the activities. Discuss the comments within your small group.

Task 2

Other members of your small group will ask you how well you thought they contributed. You should be honest and positive in your answers, looking for the good things that each member of the group did, rather than the negative ones.

Task 3

Ask your teachers/tutors to give feedback on how good they perceived your contribution to be. This will probably be given more than once, so you should gather the comments as they are given and look at them overall to get a genuine picture of yourself as your tutors see you.

Task 4

Finally, write an honest and truthful statement about your own suitability for the media industry. Draw up an action plan to make sure your skills are developed to the full.

MARKED ASSIGNMENTS

UNIT 13 – WORKING FREELANCE IN THE MEDIA INDUSTRIES

Sample assignment

Mary Hurst School

BTEC National Diploma in Media

Unit 13 :	Working Freelance in the Media Industries
Start date:	15th January
Deadline date:	6th March
Interim Assessment date:	10th February
Assessment feedback will be provided by:	11th March
Assessor:	Ken Holmes

Assignment title: Working as a freelancer in the media

Purpose

The purpose of this assignment is to provide a framework within which the learner will:

1 Understand freelance working in the media industries
2 Understand contractual obligations and financial issues in freelance work
3 Know about professional development and maintaining skills
4 Understand how to maintain workflow relevant to freelance work

Scenario

You have been asked by your local careers office to produce a report on working as a freelancer. They want to have some material for local schools to show pupils, interested in a career in the media industries, what being a freelancer is all about.

Preliminary Task

Working in a group:

a) discuss in class what being a freelancer is
b) discuss with your group the issues that are important to a freelancer
c) make notes on all these issues to use later in this assignment

The notes you take will help you to complete Tasks 2–5.

Working on your own:

Produce a report in four sections.

The first section is:

Task 1 (P1, M1, D1)

What is meant by 'working freelance' in the media industry?

In order to achieve the highest grade you must demonstrate that you have considered critically the role of freelance work. This means that you have compared this kind of work with other job roles in the media industry. You will have used supporting arguments and a range of relevant examples to demonstrate your understanding of the freelance role. You will have expressed your ideas fluently and used correct subject terminology.

The second section is:

Task 2 (P2, M2, D2)

What contractual and financial implications are there when working as a freelancer?

In order to achieve the highest grade you must demonstrate that you have critically considered the contractual and financial implications of work as a freelancer. This means that you have compared this with other contracts and finances in the media industry. You will have used supporting arguments and a range of relevant examples to demonstrate your understanding of contracts and finance. You will have expressed your ideas fluently and used correct subject terminology.

The third section is:

Task 3 (P3, M3, D3)

What are professional development and maintaining skills? Why would a freelancer need to do these things?

In order to achieve the highest grade you must demonstrate that you have critically considered professional development and maintaining skills in freelance work. This means that you have compared a range of professional development activities in the media industry. You will have used supporting arguments and a range of relevant examples to demonstrate your understanding of professional development and the need to maintain skills. You will have expressed your ideas fluently and used correct subject terminology.

The final section is:

Task 4 (P4, M4, D4)

Why is workflow important for freelancers in the media industries?

In order to achieve the highest grade you must demonstrate that you have critically considered why workflow is important for freelance work. This means that you have compared this with other job roles in the media industry. You will have used supporting arguments and a range of relevant examples to demonstrate your understanding of the freelance role. You will have expressed your ideas fluently and used correct subject terminology.

You should present your report in an appropriate way. This might be:

- **an illustrated report**
- **a presentation**
- **a mixture of both**
- **a video/audio or integrated media product.**

If you decide to undertake a presentation you must make a video or audio record of your presentation, keep presenter's notes and produce a handout for the audience.

	Grading criteria	Evidence
P1	describe the role of freelance work in the media industries expressing ideas with sufficient clarity to communicate them and with some appropriate use of subject terminology	Task 1
M1	explain the role of freelance work in the media industries with reference to well-chosen examples expressing ideas with clarity and with generally appropriate use of subject terminology	Task 1
D1	critically consider the role of freelance work in the media industries with supporting arguments and fully elucidated examples expressing ideas fluently and using subject terminology correctly	Task 1
P2	describe contractual obligations and financial issues relevant to freelance work expressing ideas with sufficient clarity to communicate them and with some appropriate use of subject terminology	Task 2
M2	explain contractual obligations and financial issues relevant to freelance work with reference to well-chosen examples expressing ideas with clarity and with generally appropriate use of subject terminology	Task 2
D2	critically consider contractual obligations and financial issues relevant to freelance work with supporting arguments and fully elucidated examples expressing ideas fluently and using subject terminology correctly	Task 2
P3	describe professional development and the maintaining of skills relevant to freelance work in the media industries expressing ideas with sufficient clarity to communicate them and with some appropriate use of subject terminology	Task 3
M3	explain professional development and the maintaining of skills relevant to freelance work in the media industries with reference to well-chosen examples expressing ideas with clarity and with generally appropriate use of subject terminology	Task 3
D3	critically consider professional development and the maintaining of skills relevant to freelance work in the media industries with supporting arguments and fully elucidated examples expressing ideas fluently and using subject terminology correctly	Task 3
P4	describe how to maintain workflow relevant to freelance work in the media industries expressing ideas with sufficient clarity to communicate them and with some appropriate use of subject terminology	Task 4
M4	explain how to maintain workflow relevant to freelance work in the media industries with reference to well-chosen examples expressing ideas with clarity and with generally appropriate use of subject terminology	Task 4
D4	critically consider aspects of workflow relevant to freelance work in the media with supporting arguments and fully elucidated examples expressing ideas fluently and using subject terminology correctly	Task 4

TASK 1 – PASS LEVEL ANSWER

Student name: Brian Wells
Task 1: What is working freelance in the media industry?
LO 1 Understand freelance working in the media industries

Media industries

The media industry has lots of sectors and they all have different ways of doing things. Freelancers work in all the media sectors in all sorts of jobs. If you are freelance you work for yourself and only get paid for each job as you do it. You may only work part of the time. You have to find the work yourself and its not like full time working for a media company where they tell you what you are doing next and you get paid whether you are working on a job or not. You have to think for yourself. You could be doing lots of different jobs as well, not just being the thing that you want to be.

Freelance media jobs

The sorts of jobs that there are will depend on if you are working in radio, TV, print, web authoring or computer games. There can be managers like producers and directors and there can be technicians like camera operators and sound recordists. You can be a designer or a writer or draw storyboards. The worst paid jobs are runners and labourers. You can work in a sector like TV or radio or you can do things for different parts of the industry if you are short of work.

Resources that freelancers need

When you get used to it you will specialise in one thing though so you will have to have the kit that you need to do the job and maybe an office and this will cost money so you can't use some one else's like at school or college.

It depends what you do like if you have to buy a proper TV camera they cast loads and then there's the lights as well. If you are an editor you will have to have your own MAC with FCP on it or your own sound recorder and mics if you are a sound man. You could rent the kit you need as you need it but then you would be paying out for that as well and it would come of your earnings. You will have to decide which is cheaper hiring or buying and reckon it in when you are deciding how much to charge.

Being a professional freelance

When you get a job your boss will want you to be professional and get the job done properly. You will have to do jobs in time to meet deadlines and be able to work when your boss wants you to work and for as long as it takes to get the job done. You mustn't let them down or not turn up for work without telling them. When you work on some jobs there may be things that you find out about some of the people that you must keep secret. A lot of information is private and must be kept private. You have to be organised and do things in the proper order without cutting corners and do a good job so you will be able to get another job. You have to be able to do more than one thing at once and this means working on one job on one day and another the next then going back to the first job on the next. It is important to work with the right people because you might find that if you work with some people it may mean you can't work with others because they are fighting for the same work. You have to be able to say what you want to say properly and write it down so they understand it.

Health and safety

When you work for yourself you have to be very careful to follow health and safety laws and work safely. You have top make sure that cables are taped down and that you don't lift too heavy equipment without getting help. You need to be fit and healthy because you don't get paid for going sick. You don't get holiday pay either which means you've got to charge more for the job so you can have time off. You've got to have your own insurance so that if you injure anyone they can get compensation.

TASK 1 – MERIT LEVEL ANSWER

Student name: Sarah Cole
Task 1: What is working freelance in the media industry?
LO 1 Understand freelance working in the media industries

Media industry sectors

The media industries is a not just one industry, but lots of related industries. They are all different types of media. They cover radio, television, film, print, web sites, CD-ROMs, computer games, journalism, and advertising. There are full time and part time jobs. Part time people are called freelancers and they have short term contracts with a company to make a product.

It's difficult being a freelancer because they have to find their own work and once the contract, is finished thy have to find another. A person who works full time for a company gets continuous work and is still paid whether they are working all the time or not.

Working as a freelance can mean that a person is only paid for the work that they do. They will probably be contracted to do a specific job, but if working full time a person may be asked to do a number of different jobs to fill in between the times when they are doing their specialist job.

Freelance specialists

A freelancer can be employed to do anything in the any of the sectors of the media industries. There are different classes of job like managers, creative jobs, technicians and labourers. Managers are the leaders like a director, producer or production manager for a radio or television programme. Creative jobs like writing, drawing & painting, storyboarding and designing, for print, radio and advertising, The technicians can be camera operators sound recorders, editors, photographers. Labourers usually do the running and cable laying jobs or are caterers

Freelancers can be specialists in one media sector like radio or television documentary, newspaper journalists, film animators or computer games designers.

Resources needed by freelancers

Freelancers will usually specialise in one part of the media which means they have to spend time on training and money on equipment, consumables and somewhere to work. A TV camera operator will probably have their own camera and lighting kit, whereas movie film makers will hire from specialist suppliers. A sound recording engineer will have to buy their own recorders and microphones. A video editor or web master will have to buy their production workstation and have an office to use it in. Writers and designers will have their office computer or laptop. Some freelancers will rent the equipment they need from a hire company and will have the cost of hire to consider when calculating how much to charge when they look for work.

Being a professional freelancer

Freelancers have to be reliable and stick to very strict deadlines so any one working in the media industry has to have a professional attitude. They need to be reliable, skilled in using equipment, and able to manage workloads. Publication and broadcast can't be changed to suit badly organised workers so freelancers have to be able to deliver. They might also be working on more than one project at once which means being organised and committed. Some projects will mean working with research into confidential issues and with people who have been suffering so there has to be understanding and privacy. It isn't always best to sell work to whoever pays the highest price because it can cause resentment with other companies. Freelance workers must be good communicators, have good presentation skills and dress for the specific job they are doing.

Health and safety issues

Freelancers like any other workers must ensure safe working practices and maintain a safe working environment for themselves and those they work with. Media work means working to deadlines so that transmission, publication and airing dates to be met. This needs a lot of self discipline and good time management skills. Fitness and good health are also essential requirements. There is no paid holiday, time off like weekends or nine to five days so rest and recreation time has to be planned into the job. A freelance worker has to arrange their own public liability insurance and other insurance and payment for pensions and illness.

TASK 1 – DISTINCTION LEVEL ANSWER

Student name: Graham Bird
Task 1: What is working freelance in the media industry?
LO1 Understand freelance working in the media industries

Sectors of the media industries

The media industries is a not really a single industry. It is a number of diverse industries each with its own recognisable working practices. The reason for categorising them together is that they are all different forms of media. Much of the material produced for radio, television, film, print, web sites, CD-ROMs, computer games, journalism, and advertising is the work of freelancers, people who enter into short term contracts with the production company to make a single product.

Being a freelancer is a precarious situation to be in. Unlike permanent employees the freelancer has to find his or her own work on a regular basis and once the contract, which may last for only a few weeks, is complete the next contract must be found. This situation is in contrast with the permanent employee who works for an employer who provides a steady workload for the employee. If an employee has nothing to do on a particular day, it doesn't affect their pay. The fluctuations in work availability are born by the employer.

The distinction between the freelancer and the independent production company is that the freelancer will often specialise in one particular task, whereas the independent production company will employ (often as freelancers) a full range of production staff.

Specialist media freelancers

The freelancer can be engaged in any capacity in the any of the sectors of the media industries. Broadly there are the following categories; manager, creator, artisan, labourer. The manager would be the creative or administrative leader like a director, producer or production manager for a radio or television programme or film, a webmaster for a web site or an editor for a newspaper. Creative jobs include writing, illustrating, like storyboarding and designing, for film, television, web sites, print publications, radio and advertising, The artisan is the individual who produces the sound or visual images according the requirements of the producer. Theses roles include camera operator, recordist and photographer. Labour intensive work can include scene shifting, runners and cable bashers.

Freelancers can also specialise in a particular type of media product like radio or television documentary, promotional and training videos, newspaper stories (journalists), animation for film or computer games that test sporting skills

Freelance resources

As stated previously most freelancers will specialise in a single aspect of media production. This will mean an investment of time and money in equipment, materials and a work space. Freelancers in different media sectors will need to invest different amounts according to their needs. A TV camera operator will often own his/her own camera and location lighting, except studio camera crews where the studio owns the kit and movie film operators who hire from specialist providers. A sound recordist will own their own recorders and microphones. A video editor CD-ROM or web author will often own the editing or authoring production workstation, which will be housed in their own premises. Writers and visual image designers will own a word processing or design computer or laptop, but the assembly process for the publication will take place on the employer's premises using their technology. Some freelancers will undoubtedly rent the technology they need from an appropriate hire company. Whichever option is chosen the cost of hire or purchase and maintenance will have to be taken into account by the freelancer in calculating how much to charge for services when pitching for work.

Freelance professionalism

All employers look for specific characteristics when recruiting for jobs and the media industry is no exception. The need to meet very strict deadlines requires that any one working in the media industry has a professional attitude to the job. Reliability, proven skills in using equipment, the ability to meet deadlines by managing workloads is crucial. Broadcasting, marketing and publication dates are fixed as much as two years in advance and the media industry freelancer has to be able to deliver often working on more than one project simultaneously. This demands a critical and ordered approach to the job. Media work often requires research into confidential documents and discussion about sensitive issues with people who have been bereaved or who are in trauma. An ethical approach must be maintained along with an ability to keep information and sources confidential. Freelancers must also ensure that they don't simply sell their work to the highest bidder as this can affect business relationships and hinder the ability to find future work. The requirement to deal with a range of commissioning producers means that the freelancer must have good communication and presentation skills and be capable of dressing appropriate to the demands of the specific job.

Health and safety for freelancers

At all time the freelancer must maintain safe working practices and be observant in maintaining a safe working environment for themselves and their colleagues. Media industry work as stated before demands work to be completed by deadlines to enable pre-planned transmission, publication and airing dates to be met. This can be stressful and calls for a high degree of self discipline, stress and time management. Physical fitness is essential and this can be enhanced by the correct diet and appropriate exercise. The freelancer doesn't get paid holiday leave or time off like weekends and nine to five days. It takes organisation and management to plan for rest and recreation. An employer will normally have in place a public liability insurance policy for all employees to guard against the risk of being sued by members of the public if anything goes wrong during the production of a media product. A freelancer must arrange their own public liability insurance and cover other risks as well like being out of work and not being able to pay the mortgage.

TASK 1 – ASSESSOR FEEDBACK

Having read the answers to the Assignment Brief, Task 1, now read the assessor's feedback. See how the learners' answers differ and what makes for a Distinction, a Merit or a Pass answer. If you are not sure of anything, check with your teacher/tutor.

Remember that this section is just as valuable whether you are studying Unit 13 yourself or not! This is because many of your assessments for a BTEC National qualification in Media will involve some written work and you will often be expected to research information when you are preparing your answers. Doing this effectively, writing clearly and concisely, preparing the work in the correct format and answering the question(s) properly are all vital skills you need to demonstrate. Getting this right early in your course will save you valuable time, help to build your confidence and enable you to gain the best grades possible from the start.

Assessor feedback P1 (including action where necessary)

Brian, you have described adequately the role of freelance work across a range of media industries, addressing specialisms, resources, professionalism and health and safety issues. You have written clearly enough to make your ideas understood and you have used some media terms appropriately.

To increase your grade to a Merit you should take more care in selecting your examples, include more clearly explained detail and use more media terms in your explanations.

Assessor feedback M1 (including action where necessary)

Sarah, you have explained well the roles of freelance work in a range of media industries including specialisms, resources, professionalism and health and safety issues, using some really good examples. Your writing is very clear and your use of media terminology is good. Sarah, you have achieved Merit.

To achieve a Distinction you should apply critical analysis techniques and provide full justification of your examples. Your use of language must be fluent and written using media terms throughout.

Assessor feedback D1

Graham, you have critically considered the roles of freelance work in a range of media industries including specialisms, resources, professionalism and health and safety issues, providing excellent examples of each. Your justification of each example is fully supported by well-reasoned argument and your writing style, which is fluent, uses media terms throughout and is an excellent piece of work. You have achieved Distinction for this learning outcome.

TASK 2 – PASS LEVEL ANSWER

TASK 2
Student name: Hillary Craig
Task 2: What contractual and financial implications are there for working as a freelancer?
LO2 Understand contractual obligations and financial issues in freelance work

---

Freelance contracts

If you work freelance you will have a contract that will tell you what you have to do for the job a bit like some one who has a full time job except their contract will not go into the detail of each individual job like yours will. There will be a date for getting the job done by and a list of what you have to do for the job. There might be a penalty clause that means that if you miss the deadline you don't get as much money. If you don't finish a job because you are sick you won't get paid. All freelance contracts have to be agreed separately and they usually start with someone advertising for people to do the job. It's called commissioning and it's different in different media sectors. There are rules to follow and you can't just make a media product and send it to a company hoping they will publish or broadcast it. You will get a brief and you will have to show the company that you can do the job before they will give you a contract. You must know about copyright and who has copyright on what.

Payment for freelance work

You can be paid all at once or given different amounts as you do each part of the work. You might have to send an invoice for the work you've done or it might come automatically. Sometimes you may have to wait for your money and this means you have to have enough to live on while you wait which can be a problem if you've paid out for kit hire to do the job. You might even have to borrow from your bank until you get paid. Then there is income tax and national insurance to think about. If you are in a full time job tax, sickness and pension money is taken off your money before you get your wage so you don't have to worry. You will also have to pay for insurance in case any one claims that you injured them while you are working. Working for yourself means that you have to arrange all these things yourself. You might have to open accounts with suppliers to get credit so you will have enough cash to live on while you are waiting to get paid.

TASK 2 – MERIT LEVEL ANSWER

Student name: Etusha Patel
Task 2: What contractual and financial implications are there for working as a freelancer?
LO2 Understand contractual obligations and financial issues in freelance work

---

Freelance working contracts

Contractual obligations apply to freelance workers just as to full time employees except that a freelance contract is more specific and detailed being related only to the job that has been contracted. Full time contracts cover working hours, holiday benefits and notice required. They will also have a job description that lists the employee's general duties which can be changed as the company needs change.

A freelance contract will state the completion date of the specific job, the details of the job and the standard of work that is expected. There might be a bonus clause payable on doing the work by the deadline or a penalty clause withholding payment or part payment if not done in time or well enough. If the work can't be completed because of illness or circumstances beyond their control no payment will be made.

Freelance contracts usually are agreed through negotiation and the freelancer tries to get the best deal they can. This is done when the commissioning happens. The process may be different depending on the sector and the company that produces the product. In television there are three commissioning processes depending on the company. The BBC has a list of independent production companies for TV and radio that it will deal with on its web site, or by contacting the commissioning editor of the relevant BBC network if you have an idea for a programme. Channel 4 will accept TV shorts just by sending them in.

The print sector is easier for getting freelance work. There is an accepted way of submitting an idea and a sample of a book for publication and journalists can do work individually to write articles for newspapers and magazines.

Freelancers will always work to a brief that has been commissioned by a production company. A brief will state the target audience, topic and size of the product to be made. Books or articles for a magazines or newspapers will have a word and page count, number and size of illustrations and clearance money. TV or radio programmes will have to comply with criteria like running time, topic and target audience. Copyright clearance arrangements will be stated. Websites and interactive CD-ROMs will be commissioned by a company for which they are being produced.

In any case the brief will specify the detail of the product and the freelancer or production company for whom the freelancer works will have to respond to the brief with a proposal. The freelancer will do a detailed treatment and budget showing exactly how the product will be made and what it will contain. If location filming or recording is required the schedules will include a risk assessment.

Copyright and intellectual property rights need to be agreed before a media product is commissioned. Material that is used in a media product whether it is music, lyric, text, moving or still image if it is produced by some one else must have the permission of the owner of the copyright before it can be reproduced in a media product. MCPS, PRS and PPL cover audio copyright. Newsreel and clipping libraries hold copyright on visual resources and copyright on extracts from radio and TV programmes and films is usually owned by the makers of the product.

Getting paid as a freelancer

Freelancers get paid either on completion or in two or more instalments and will be agreed as part of the contract when commissioned to produce the product. Sometimes payment is automatic and other times invoices have to be sent. Some companies only pay out every year or are late in settling which can cause problems with cash flow because there are still the regular payments to be met by the freelancer.

These can include rent for premises and equipment, tax invoices national insurance, VAT and so on. Insurance premiums sickness and pension contributions will also need to be paid. There are other casts to consider like paying an accountant to work out and complete tax returns and the cost of a business account with the bank. It may be necessary to open accounts with suppliers to increase the amount of working capital that the freelancer has at their disposal.

TASK 2 – DISTINCTION LEVEL ANSWER

Student name: Nicola Briant
Task 2: What contractual and financial implications are there for working as a freelancer?
LO2 Understand contractual obligations and financial issues in freelance work

---

Freelance contracts

The freelancer is generally subject to contractual obligations just the same as a permanent employee except that the contract of employment for a permanent employee will be more generalised than that of a freelance worker. Permanent employee contracts will state weekly hours, number of weeks holiday, sickness and other entitlements, period of notice required and given for termination. Public sector contracts will state collective bargaining terms for renegotiating salary. The permanent contract is usually used in conjunction with a person specification that will state the required skills, experience and education required to do the job and a job description that will explain in more detail what the employee will do from day to day.

Freelance contracts on the other hand will specify the completion date of the specific job for which the freelancer has been contracted, the specific details of the job and the quality of work that is required. There will often be a clause stating that a bonus will be payable on completion by the specified deadline or a penalty clause stating that no payment will be made unless the work is of an appropriate quality. No payment will be made for example if the work can't be completed due to the freelancer being ill or unable to complete because of circumstances beyond their control. (This is why insurance is required, see above.)

Freelance contracts have to be negotiated and sometimes it is possible to agree better terms than the original contract was offering if there are extenuating circumstances like a much tighter deadline than would be usual, or if there is an unexpected event to be covered. In freelance media work the freelancer is often commissioned to produce a product. This commissioning process varies according to the sector and in some sectors according to the company that distributes the product. In television for example the three major broadcasters BBC, ITC and channel 4 each have their own commissioning process with specific variations. The BBC has approved lists of independent production companies that are drawn up and available on their web site. Only companies listed can pitch for commissions to make programmes. This also applies to BBC radio. The only way that a freelancer can obtain work from the BBC is by contacting either one of the independent production companies or by contacting the commissioning editor of the relevant BBC network. Even then it is usually to offer an idea for a production rather than to actually obtain a freelance contract to produce a programme. Channel 4 on the other hand will accept work particularly TV shorts that have been produced without prior consultation.

Working in the print sector is perhaps easier for obtaining freelance work. Journalists will often work individually to a freelance contract to produce a series of articles or an author will write a book for a publisher as a freelance writer.

Working as a freelancer will inevitably mean working to a commissioned brief. This means that the commissioning editor will put out a specification for a particular media product, stating the target audience, the topic and the size of the product to be made. A book or article for a magazine or newspaper will have a predetermined word and page count, total number and size of illustrations and a maximum amount of money set aside for copyright clearance of third party images. A TV or radio programme will have to conform to specified criteria like running time, topic and target audience. The style of titling and credits will also be set by the commissioner. Clearance of copyright images will also need to be paid for. Websites and interactive CD-ROMs are usually commissioned by a client or company for which they are being produced and the tendering process may well be used by the client to obtain the best deal.

In all cases the brief will specify the detail of what the customer wants the product to look like and the freelancer or production company for whom the freelancer works will have to respond to the brief with a proposal that will include the costing and which must be approved by the client. Following this the freelancer will produce a detailed treatment and budget breakdown showing exactly how the product will be made and what it will contain. The freelancer will be expected to plan the production process from beginning to end and draw up a full production schedule to enable the commissioner to see when each stage of the process will be complete. If location filming or recording is required the schedules will include a full risk assessment to ensure the safety of those working on the product, particularly if the is to be subcontracting of work to third parties, which is likely for television, film and radio. Where third parties are engaged to contribute to books there will not be the same issues of safety at work because writers generally don't work in high risk work places, but it may be necessary to take out some form of insurance to cover unforeseen illness or negligence in submitting work by the copy date stated in the contract.

Issues of copyright and intellectual property rights need to be agreed prior to a media product being commissioned. Generally any third party material that is used in a media product whether it is music, lyric, text, moving or still image recorded by whatever means must have the permission of the owner of the copyright of that work, before it can be reproduced in a media product. It is not always the case that clearance will be given, in which case a substitute must be found. Organisations like MCPS, PRS and PPL cover audio copyright. Newsreel and clipping libraries hold copyright on vast visual resources and copyright on extracts from radio and TV programmes and films is usually owned by the makers of the product.

Intellectual property rights can exist in anything but usually in written work, like the content of books. The ownership of the text of a book or and article in a magazine or newspaper is decided prior to the writing of the text and can either be transferred to the publisher or retained by the author.

Getting paid as a freelancer

Payment for freelance work can be made in stages or on completion of the commission. This will be agreed as part of the contract that results from being commissioned to produce the product. Some broadcasters, publishers or retailers will require an account to be submitted while others will pay automatically on acceptance of the work. Payment may not however be prompt and some media companies will only pay one or twice a year. This can leave the freelancer with a cash flow problem while waiting for payment and if there are overheads like mortgages, office and equipment rental to be paid before production can go ahead, the freelancer may well have to borrow money at interest to cover these costs.

Income tax and national insurance also have to be paid by the freelancer. Income tax is usually paid retrospectively on an annual basis, whereas National insurance can be purchased weekly. The freelancer will also need to purchase public liability insurance if working in a situation where they come into contact with the public, like on a TV shoot and although a freelancer may be young the issue of saving for a pension must be considered and money put aside, because the state doesn't provide for the self-employed in the same way as it does for those in conventional employment. Other overheads include paying for the services of an accountant to work out the expenses and allowances that can be offset against tax and tom work out the amount of tax that will be payable to the revenue. It is usual to have a business bank account for which there is a charge and the bank will require an acceptable business plan to be submitted prior to agreeing to authorise one. The need for the provision of working capital could require that the bank provides an authorised overdraft facility. This will be part of the structured business plan. Accounts will need to be opened with appropriate suppliers to increase the amount of working capital that the freelancer has at their disposal.

TASK 2 – ASSESSOR FEEDBACK

As with Task 1, compare the way the different learners have completed Task 2 and see what it takes to produce work at Distinction and Merit level rather than Pass. Apply this to your own work. If you are not sure of anything, ask your teacher/tutor.

Assessor feedback P2 (including action where necessary)

Hillary, you have adequately, if superficially, written about general contractual and financial issues relevant to working freelance in any sector of the media industries. You writing is clear enough for your ideas to be understood and you have used some media terms.

To get a Merit you must identify some good examples from appropriate sectors of the industry, going into greater detail and explanation of why they are written. Your writing needs to be clearer and your use of media jargon should be greater.

Assessor feedback M2 (including action where necessary)

Etusha, you have explained well the specific contractual obligations and financial issues relevant to freelance working in the media industries, making reference to a good selection of examples. You have a good writing style that enables you to express your ideas clearly and you have used mainly appropriate media language.

To get a Distinction you will need to be critically analytical in your writing and provide fully justified arguments for your examples. You need also to write more fluently using media terms throughout.

Assessor feedback D2

Nicola, you have critically considered contractual obligations and financial issues relevant to freelancers in a range of media industries, providing excellent examples of specific roles. Your justification of each example is fully supported by well-reasoned argument and your writing style, which is fluent, uses media terms throughout and is an excellent piece of work. You have achieved Distinction.

TASK 3 – PASS LEVEL ANSWER

Student name: Charlie Webster
Task 3: What are professional development and maintaining skills – why would a freelancer need to do these things?
LO 3 Know about professional development and maintaining skills

It is important for freelancers to have qualifications. This may be:

- National Diploma – from college
- Degree – from university
- NVQ – from the workplace

Freelancers need to show an employer or client that they are qualified in some way. They also need to keep up to date with what is happening in the media. They should think about taking further qualifications even though they thought they know it all.

Having experience of working in the media is also important. You have to show an employer or client that you have some skills in the area you work in. Gaining experience is not easy. Maybe you can work part time for a company or event work for free. Sometimes professionals have to update their skills and they can do this by working for someone for free.

Professional bodies are important because they provide information and support for freelancers. Skillset provide support for freelancers through their training grants available to freelancers. You have to have a background in media and other factors are taken into consideration when applying for training funds. However, it is possible to apply and receive support from them. There are other professional bodies such as:

- British Institute of Professional Photographer
- The Institute of Videography

It might cost money to be a member of a professional body but there can be benefits. They may be able to recommend you to clients and you could achieve letters after your name if you qualify for full membership.

Strengths and weaknesses

Freelancers have to consider what they are good at what they are not so good at. This means that they can consider how to get good at the things they do not do so well. This might be IT and freelancers need to use IT to maintain contact with other freelancers, employers and clients. It may be that a freelancer has limited skills in video editing using a computer. There are plenty of companies offering training so they need to identify this.

Freelancers should undertake a regular review of their strengths and weaknesses using a suitable method. There are many of these and freelancer should look carefully at what is best for them.

Here is a list of some of the skills updating opportunities available to freelancers:

- Going to a local college for evening classes
- Going to a university to undertake a new qualification – eg. Higher National Diploma (full time)
- Going to a college or university to undertake a part time qualification – eg Higher National Certificate or Short Course

Freelancers should look at websites in order to find updating opportunities

Freelancers must maintain the skills they already have. They can do this by undertaking regular work in their specialist area. They could also talk to other freelancers about what they do.

Freelancers need to have qualifications, as discussed earlier, and these qualifications can be to update previous skills. For example;

A freelance video camera operator has been using tape based DVCAM cameras for five years. They are used to using a camera that is standard screen rather than wide screen. They need to see how shooting in wide screen is different to normal screen.

They could undertake some learning by attending a course run by a local college in the evenings. This will give them new skills in using wide screen cameras. They could work with a colleague who has a wide screen camera and go with them on location so that they can understand how to compose a picture using wide screen. They could look at websites forums where professionals share their knowledge through the internet. They could join a professional body where they could get advice from other professionals eg. the Institute of Videographers where they have a forum and other camera people talk to each other about their cameras.

There are a number of part-time courses for updating skills such as:

- Level 4 BTEC Professional Certificate in Digital Video
- Level 4 BTEC Professional Certificate in Digital Audio Editing
- Level 4 BTEC Professional Certificate in Video Journalism
- Level 4 BTEC Professional Certificate in Web Publishing

Freelancers would need to find a college or university near to them that offers this qualification. They may be able to do a qualification like this through distance learning working at home and sending in their work by post.

It is important for freelancers to make time for professional development. If they are to move on in the industry they have to keep up to date with what is happening and the skills they need.

TASK 3 – MERIT LEVEL ANSWER

Student name: Dwayne Cramer
Task 3: What are professional development and maintaining skills – why would a freelancer need to do these things?
LO 3 Know about professional development and maintaining skills

A freelancer working in the media industries has to know what their skills are and what they need to learn about. Media technology is constantly changing as freelancers must be understand and be able to use this new technology. For example, the technology of recording sound has changed dramatically over the past few years. A sound recordist trained to use a Uher recorder on location would have been sought after for both radio and television work. Being able to record sound from two or more sources onto a professional reel to reel recorder was seen as the ultimate in professional sound recording. Now sound recordists can use a digital recorder that is probably 50% smaller than a Uher and has the capability to record multiple sound tracks that can then be transferred almost instantaneously to a computer. A sound recordist would need to know about this technology and be able to use it.

How does a freelancer find out about changes in technology and media practice?

This may come from undertaking a qualification provided by a professional body such as the Association of Professional Recording Services (APRS).

The APRS is dedicated to promoting the highest standards throughout the sound recording industry. Its board of directors are all working professionals in this area. They provide training as stated on their website:

The APRS and the MPG have combined their educational efforts to create JAMES (Joint Audio Media Education Services), set up to support Education and Training.

The JAMES Committee considers training and education to be the vitally important means to nurture tomorrow's talent, promote ever higher standards and to ensure that the many years of industry experience are not lost to future generations.

This is a quote from one of pages on their training site. This is about one university and the range of equipment they use for training in sound recording:

'The facilities at Leeds Met were frankly superb. Their two large Munro Associates Studios would not be out of place in any professional facility. In addition, they boast another four Munro control rooms and four more live rooms, two of which are dedicated to Foley and ADR.'

Freelancers need to know about the range of qualifications and training that could be available to them.

Another professional body for sound recordists is the Institute of Broadcast Sound (IBS).

The IBS was founded in 1977 by sound balancers in radio and television. Members can have their details on the database of sound recordists for potential employers or clients to see. They have regularly updated information about the industry that helps their members to keep abreast of changes in technology and the media industries.

Skilset is the Skills Sector Council for the Audio Visual Industry. They have funds available for freelancers to update their skills. A typical course they offer is Skillset have developed a Skills Strategy for the UK Radio Industry. They are working with The Radio Academy to identify and promote best practice in training and development in the radio industry.

Freelancers should look at all these initiatives in order to update their knowledge of the industry and to see how they might be funded for further training

It is vitally important for freelancers to maintain the skills they have and gain new skills. They can maintain skills by undertaking freelance jobs that allow them to do what they are good at. They must also consider how they can develop their skills. This might not be easy in a very cut throat industry. It has been said that there is always someone waiting to take your job in the media industry. This can be very true but a good freelancer will always be in demand.

Freelancers must find time for developing their skills. This might be through:

- On the job training – doing an NVQ qualification whilst working as freelance sound recordist. This is generally achieved by undertaking work and completing tasks that prove you are able to do the work.
- Short courses – this could be anything from two weeks to a year and may be full or part time. Id it was full time a freelancer would have to consider how much money they would loose by not being able to work. They would balance this against how much more they could earn with new skills.
- Distance learning – this involve studying at home and attending workshops and sending in work for assessment. This can be good for freelancers as they can continue to work and study.

Of course freelancers can learn by studying what other professionals can do. This means that they have to keep careful notes on techniques and technology used by professionals and maybe asking if they can try to use it.

Professional bodies can offer support to freelancers as I stated earlier. Freelancers must weigh up the cost of membership against the benefits they might receive. If they are on the bodies database they might receive lots of work, offers of further training and advice from other professionals in the same organisation.

TASK 3 – DISTINCTION LEVEL ANSWER

Student name: Fara Khan
Task 3: What are professional development and maintaining skills – why would a freelancer need to do these things?
LO 3 Know about professional development and maintaining skills

It is important for media professionals to undertake professional development. The technology in media is constantly changing so it is important to keep up to date with these changes. Manu colleges and universities offer professional development course so that media professionals can update their skills.

Working as a freelancer can provide a wide range of skills as you are able to move between companies and do different jobs. However, there is not always the security of having a regular job. One day you can be a runner on a feature film and the next day making tea for a client.

Being a member of a professional body can help with training as they will advise you on where you can go to update your skills. I have looked at the British Institute of Professional Photographers who offer professional development courses for their members. These include courses on:

- Lighting for fashion
- Stock library
- Digital Photoshop
- Marketing

The BIPP has a search engine that allows clients to find a professional photographer in their area. This would be really helpful for a freelance photographer who signs up for membership. Only qualified photographers can be members so that they can reassure clients that their members will do a good job.

A media professional has to understand what their strengths and weakness are. If they are to move on the industry they have to realise what they are good at and what skills they need to develop. One way to do this is to undertake a SWOT analysis. This involves looking at four different aspects of yourself and seeing what you can change. This is an example of a SWOT analysis form

Strengths	Weaknesses
Opportunities	Threats

Each of these areas should be considered and analysed in order to formulate a plan for developing your weaknesses and further developing your strengths. Media professionals cannot stand still; they have to look to the future if they are to survive in the media industry.

A good point to start to look at professional development is the Skillset website. Skillset is the Sector Skills Council for the Audio Visual industries.

This is a quote from their website:

Skillset is the Sector Skills Council for the Audio Visual Industries (broadcast, film, video, interactive media and photo imaging). Jointly funded by industry and government, our job is to make sure that the UK audio visual industries have the right people, with the right skills, in the right place, at the right time, so that our industries remain competitive.

Source: www.skillset.org.uk

Skillset offer training called Screen Bursary and this can help professionals in the audio visual industry to gain new skills.

I think that a freelancer undertake regular professional development if they are to stay ahead of the game. If they want more work and gain a good reputation they need to consider how they might acquire new skills and what these skills need to be.

It is important for media professionals working as freelancers to maintain skills. It is often difficult to find time to review the ways in which the media industry is changing. It must be difficult for people who have been working in the film industry to understand how the technology of, for example, editing has changed. The days of cutting up film has now been replaced by computer technology.

Freelancers should receive trade publications regularly. Many of these are free, for example:

Audio Visual Magazine
The Producer
High Definition Magazine
Audio Media
Televisual

There are also paid for publications such as Broadcast – a weekly magazine for the broadcast industry.

There are a number of professional bodies in the media industry. Earlier I talked about The BIPP. There are many more that work in particular media industries. For example:

Commercial Radio Companies Association	*The role of the RadioCentre is to maintain and build a strong and successful Commercial Radio industry — both in terms of listening hours and revenues. As such, the RadioCentre operates in a number of areas including working with advertisers and their agencies, working with government, Ofcom and policy makers, and also stations themselves* Source: www.radiocentre.org
Independent Publishers Guild	The IPG supports around 480 members who have a combined turnover of £500m a year and who make enormous contributions to creative excellence and innovation in the UK. We supply our members with vital information, practical advice and great ideas to help them grow and prosper. We represent their interests in the wider publishing industry. And we provide a friendly community in which independent publishers can share knowledge and experiences. Source: www.ipg.uk.com/
Producer's Alliance for Cinema and Television	*Pact is the UK trade association that represents and promotes the commercial interests of independent feature film, television, animation and interactive media companies. Headquartered in London, Pact has regional representation throughout the UK, in order to support its members.* Source: www.pact.co.uk
Broadcasting Entertainment Cinematography and Theatre Union	*BECTU is the independent union for those working in broadcasting, film, theatre, entertainment, leisure, interactive media and allied areas* Source: www.bectu.org.uk

Media professionals can use these associations to find information about their area of the media industry.

It is, of course, valuable to learn new skills from other professionals. Working as a freelancer puts you in contact with many professionals as you move from job to job. A freelancer should always ask questions and find answers from someone who knows.

Freelance personnel need to maintain their skills by undertaking professional development n the right way. It would be no good going out and spending lots of money on a course if this course was not going to increase skills.

I think that if I was freelance camera operator I would want to look at the latest technology. This will be High Definition television and I would want to be at the forefront of this technology. A camera operator that knows about HD and can operate an HD camera has got to be worth employing. Freelancers can not stick their heads in the sand and hope that new technology will go away – it won't!

TASK 3 – ASSESSOR FEEDBACK

Check that you know why Fara's work was graded as Distinction and Charlie's is only Pass.

Assessor feedback P3 (including action where necessary)
Charlie, you have provided a basic description of professional development and maintaining skills. You have expressed your ideas with sufficient detail and you use some appropriate subject terminology. You could have used illustrations to aid your descriptions and chosen more professional bodies to discuss. Your work is quite limited in content and depth. **In order to gain a higher grade** you must move from simple description to an explanation or critical consideration. You should use a wider range of examples that could be across a wider range of media sectors. You should use appropriate subject terminology and make your answer easy to read and fluent.
Assessor feedback M3 (including action where necessary)
Dwayne, you explained professional development and maintaining skills clearly and included some relevant examples and illustrations. Your examples were well chosen and explained clearly. You have demonstrated that you have a good understanding of professional development and maintaining skills in one area of the media. Your use of subject terminology was generally appropriate, with some lapses. You should have included more examples from a wider range of media industries. **In order to gain a Distinction** you will have to include information about other media areas using a higher level of subject terminology.
Assessor feedback D3
Fara, you have provided an extensive and illustrated critical consideration of professional development. You have analysed and justified your discussion with clear examples across a range of media areas. You have identified a range of ways in which media professionals can maintain their skills. These are carefully targeted at freelancers in the media industry. You have used fluent language in this report and you have used illustrations to illuminate your discussion. You have used correct subject terminology throughout your work.

TASK 4 – PASS LEVEL ANSWER

TASK 4
Student name: Josie Wilkinson
Task 4: Why is workflow important for freelancers in the media industries?
LO 4 Understand how to maintain workflow relevant to freelance work

---

Freelancers need to keep a constant flow of work. If they do not they might find that they have no money to pay their bills. Freelancers might have to buy their own equipment and if they do not make any money this will be impossible.

If they want to maintain workflow they will have to:

- Be able to sell themselves through a website – maybe get a friend to design one for them.
- Find an agent who will get them work – this costs money so must be cost effective
- Read trade journals – this might provide some contacts
- Go to trade events – they might be able to meet people and give them a business card
- Networking – this could be a circle of friends who talk to each other about being a freelancer and share experiences
- Word of mouth – sometimes people hear about what a good job you have done and contact you. This a very cost effective way of getting work

Freelancers have to market themselves. They should consider;

- Having some business cards printed – this can be quite expensive unless you use a web based printer or do you own cards
- Use the website they have developed to put examples of their work and then tell people how to get on to the site
- Producing a CV that can be put on website or sent out to potential clients or employers
- Preparing a showreel or portfolio that can be shown to employers or clients – this could be put on a website such as YouTube or they could register with Facebook
- Network through Facebook or other social sites to get their name known
- Preparing a press release and send it to local and national papers and trade magazines
- Producing a promotional flyer or brochure to send to employers or clients
- Attending a film festival and handing our their business cards, flyers or brochures

- Entering a film for a festival so that they may get a prize and recognised by a major film producer

Freelancers need to get some feedback from clients. This can then be used to demonstrate to potential clients how good they are. They should ask clients to provide them with a reference that states how well they worked and how good their product was. They will also need some feedback from their peers. This might be feedback on how well they worked with other people as much media work is undertaken in teams.

Freelancers must undertake self-review in order to see where they are going and what they need to do next. It is very easy to simply go along without learning something new. They need to see just what they need to learn in order to move on the next phase of their career.

TASK 4 – MERIT LEVEL

Student name: Zin Zue
Task 4: Why is workflow important for freelancers in the media industries?
LO 4 Understand how to maintain workflow relevant to freelance work

---

Understand how to maintain workflow relevant to freelance work

Zin Zue

Maintaining work flow

Websites

A freelancer could have a website that demonstrates what they can do

Maintaining work flow

Agents and agencies

Freelancers can arrange to be on the books of an agent

These people find work for freelancers and they take a commission

Maintaining work flow

Agents and agencies

Freelancers can arrange to be on the books of an agent

These people find work for freelancers and they take a commission

Maintaining work flow

Networking

Freelancers must have a network of contacts.

This might be through past jobs or recommendations

Maintaining work flow

It is important to maintain a network through regular contact

Freelancers should be IT literate and be able to use a computer for emails and a mobile phone for texts

Marketing yourself

Freelancers should be able to 'sell' themselves to a potential employer

To do this they could:

Marketing yourself

Produce business cards – companies such as Vistaprint do this for a small fee

Make a website – if they do not know how to do this they should ask a colleague

Marketing yourself

A freelancer needs to produce an accurate CV.

This should show all the jobs / roles undertaken and when these took place.

The CV can also demonstrate what skills a freelancer has

Marketing yourself

A show reel or portfolio can be sent to a potential employer or client

This should demonstrate best work

Marketing yourself

Finally

A freelancer should take every oportunity to get themselves know

This could be through:

Marketing yourself

- Producing a press release
- Making some promotional material – a flyer, brochure or DVD
- Visiting festivals and meeting people
- Presenting their work for exhibitions or competitions

Self-assessment

It is always good to get feedback from clients

This could be used in promotional material

It can also be a reference for you when meeting new clients or employers

Self-assessment

It is also good to get feedback from peers.

This might be colleagues you have worked with

Their views can be used to demonstrate how you work as a team member

Self-assessment

It is important to take time to review yourself and see just where you are and what you want to do

Think about the SWOT analysis and see what you need to do to make it as a freelancer!

TASK 4 – DISTINCTION LEVEL ANSWER

Student name: Marion Bremner
Task 4: Why is workflow important for freelancers in the media industries?
LO 4 Understand how to maintain workflow relevant to freelance work

---

Understand Freelance Workflow

Marion Bremner

Understand Freelance Workflow

Freelancers need to maintain a steady workflow in order to survive in the media industries

Working for a few days and then not working for a few weeks is not a good idea

Understand Freelance Workflow

You can see from the following graph that income must exceed expenditure if a freelancer is to succeed and survive

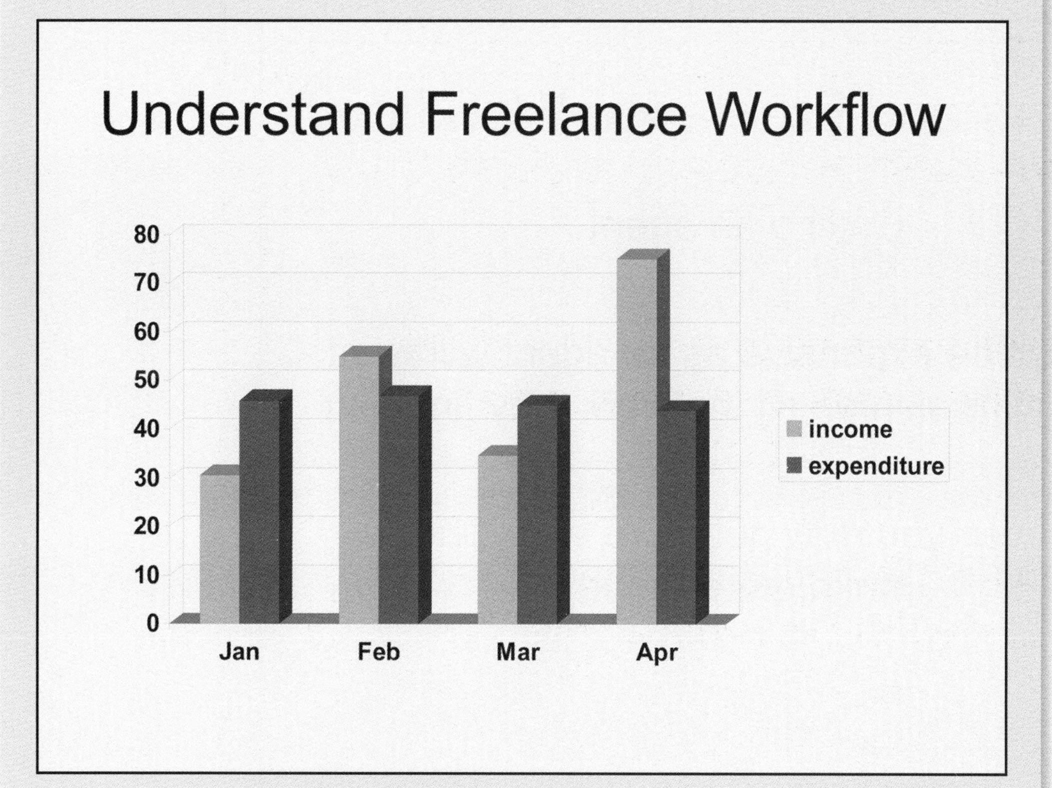

Understand Freelance Workflow

A freelancer needs to maintain a steady flow of work. This could be achieved by:

Understand Freelance Workflow

Getting an agent

This can be expensive as an agent will want a commission on all the work they find you

However, you may get more work and so make more money

Understand Freelance Workflow

Building a website

This can be a good way of showing what you can do.

It will have to look good and work well if you want people to know that you are a professional

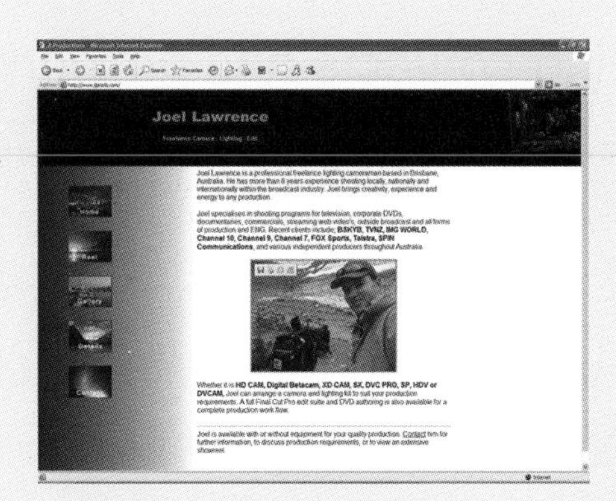

Understand Freelance Workflow

Trade Journals such as;

Broadcast (paid for) and Televisual (free to media professionals) provide details of new technology and techniques

Understand Freelance Workflow

Maintaining contacts and networking are essential for freelancers

Some jobs can come by word of mouth and without your name being known you may never get this job

Understand Freelance Workflow

Freelancers need to market themselves.

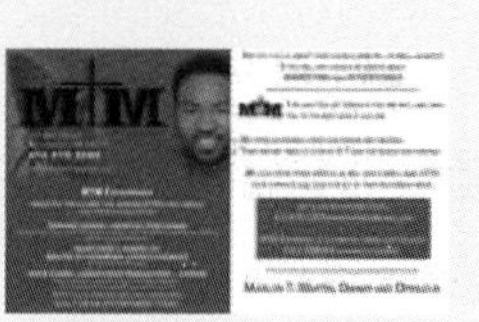

They could produce a business card

or a brochure

Understand Freelance Workflow

A freelancer will need:

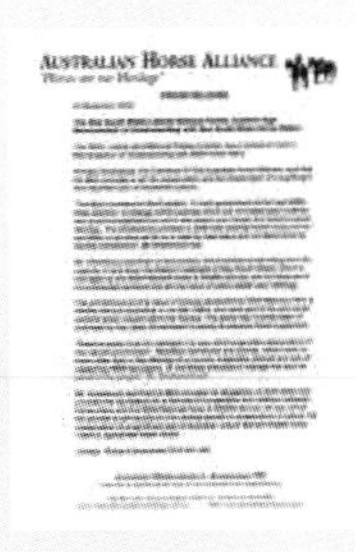

AUSTRALIAN HORSE ALLIANCE

A CV

Press releases

Understand Freelance Workflow

A good way to get your work seen is to make a show reel or portfolio

This can be sent to prospective employers or clients to demonstrate your skills

Understand Freelance Workflow

Why not make a short film and enter it for a competition

You never know who might see your film and ask you to work for them

Understand Freelance Workflow

Self Assessment

It is important for freelancers to get some feedback from clients. This can be used to review your own performance and will give you material to use on your promotional material

Understand Freelance Workflow

Here are some examples of quotes:

'The best short film I have seen in a long time'

'Marion was always on time and worked really hard'

'Marion showed great creativity when working on this project'

Understand Freelance Workflow

Self Assessment

It is also important to get feedback from peers. This will allow you to see how your peers see you and how you work as team member

Being a team member is important in the media industries

Understand Freelance Workflow

As you can see it is essential for a freelancer to:

- Maintain relevant workflow
- Find clients
- Market themselves effectively
- Review their work
- Be reliable and effective as a freelancer

Understand Freelance Workflow

Being a freelancer in the media industries can be one of the best jobs in the world

This is a quote from a freelancer
' I love this job as I get to do so many different things and work with some really talented people'

Understand Freelance Workflow

Biography

Images – Google uk
Quote – PMH Productions website

TASK 4 – ASSESSOR FEEDBACK

Check with your teacher/tutor if you are not clear why each student gained the grade he or she did.

Assessor feedback P4 (including action where necessary)

Josie, your work covers the criterion by describing workflow but it lacks a range of well-chosen examples. It almost reads as a list. You should have included examples of agents, networks and marketing methods. These could have been illustrated with examples from the Internet.
In order to gain a higher grade you must produce well-chosen examples to illustrate your work. You must use fluent and appropriate subject terminology. Why not think about using a presentation with illustrations? We discussed this before you started your work but you seem to have ignored this.

Assessor feedback M4 (including action where necessary)

Zin, you have explained how to maintain a workflow using an appropriate presentation technique. Your ideas are expressed clearly and you have demonstrated some use of appropriate subject terminology. Your presentation lacks illustration and this makes it rather dull. You did present your evidence in an appropriate way, although you could have interacted more with the audience. You provided a handout and you were able to answer some questions at the end of the presentation.
In order to achieve a Merit you should provide a more critical account of workflow with comparisons across the media sectors. Your subject terminology must be correct at all times.

Assessor feedback D4

Marion, you have chosen to submit your work as a presentation. It is clear that you have an excellent understanding of workflow and have made this relevant to media freelancers. The PowerPoint slides are well illustrated and clear. You have covered the major areas of why it is important for freelancers to have a constant flow of work. The slides were complemented by a handout that was given to the audience. Your presentation was excellent and you spoke to the audience rather than at the slides. The presentation was recorded on video. Your use of subject terminology was excellent, as was your fluent development of your ideas and examples. You have achieved Distinction level.